THE TEMECULA MASSACRE

THE TEMECULA MASSACRE

A FORGOTTEN BATTLEFIELD LANDSCAPE OF THE MEXICAN-AMERICAN WAR

GARY P. DUBOIS AND LISA L. WOODWARD

Great Oak Press
Pechanga, California

Cover photograph: *Indian Graveyard at Temecula.* Frederic Hamer Maude Collection, Catalog number: SCWHR-P-002.2-2426R. Seaver Center for Western History Research, Los Angeles County Museum of Natural History.

Cover and interior designer: Ashley Halsey
Managing editor: Molly McGrath

ISBN: 978-1-942279-39-6 (hardcover)

Library of Congress Control Number: 2024933257
Printed in the United States of America.

Great Oak Press
P.O. Box 1477
Temecula, CA, 92593
www.greatoakpress.com

Móltavannaat Pecháangayam Póomik

Dedicated to the Pechanga People

CONTENTS

FOREWORD

The Temecula Massacre: A Forgotten Battlefield Landscape of the Mexican-American War is a historical record of the death, displacement, dispossession, and reclamation of the Native people who died during one of the deadliest conflicts of the Mexican-American War. The aim of this book is to raise awareness of this overlooked battle of United States and California history, to recognize the historically significant massacre, and to introduce the modern-day movement toward preservation of the battlefield, landscape, and the Temecula Indian Cemetery, Pávkun.

The Pechanga Band of Indians are the keepers of key information regarding these events, and this work is the culmination of traditional Tribal knowledge and primary historical documents. This book contains a multifaceted interpretation of the sequence of events surrounding the massacre and the consequences of the battle. Much of the contents of this book is new information from Tribal sources that has never been shared or interconnected with published historic accounts of the Battle of San Pasqual and the Temecula Massacre. Supplemental maps, ethnographic notes and sound recordings, and photographs assist with the documentation to provide a more complete account of these events. A documentary film, offering a summarized version of the content of this book, is also available.

The Temecula Massacre: A Forgotten Battlefield Landscape of the Mexican-American War is meant to accompany this auxiliary material or may stand alone as a classroom or library textbook. The authors invite anyone who is interested in learning the fuller history of California's entry to the Union to read this account and thereby learn of the importance of Native people's involvement then and now.

SCAN ME

ACKNOWLEDGMENTS

THIS BOOK WAS WRITTEN TO HONOR the victims of the Temecula Massacre and is dedicated to the descendants of the people who lost their lives during this tragic event. As the years go by, the memory of the Massacre slips further from the consciousness of the community and we believe it is important to document it, not only for the Pechanga Tribal community but for all who live in the Temecula Valley. We would like to thank our spouses and children for their support and encouragement during the writing of this book. We are indebted to Monica Wilson, an exceptional researcher who tracked down some of the most obscure maps and references and assisted with the compilation of the account. Filmmaker, Daniel Golding found photos and images that help tell the story visually and Pechanga Tribal Chairman, Mark Macarro, shared accounts only known through the oral tradition, providing information from the Native perspective that is not found in any primary or published sources. We also want to thank the Pechanga Tribal Council for supporting and assisting this project.

TIMELINE OF EVENTS

Time Immemorial	For the 'Atáaxum (Luiseño), the Creation of the World occurs at 'Éxva Teméeku. The archaeological record confirms continuous occupation of the Temecula Valley for over 10,000 years.
1769	Father Junípero Serra arrives in Alta California and establishes the San Diego Mission.
1798	Mission San Luis Rey is established in Oceanside, California.
1821	Mexico achieves independence from Spain.
1834	Secularization of the Missions.
1843	Pablo Apis a native of Waxáwmay (Guajome) Village near San Luis Rey Mission receives the Little Temecula Rancho.
1844	• José Antonio Serrano receives the Pauma Rancho land grant.

1844 *cont.*

- Isaac Williams establishes a relationship with the Apis family and secures Luiseño laborers for his cattle enterprise.
- Jonathan Trumbull Warner receives the Rancho Valle de San José and establishes Warner Ranch.

1845 Governor Pío Pico formally confirms Pablo Apis' land grant, Little Temecula Rancho, which he received in 1843.

1846 Temecula Indian María Antonia Apis has four children by Isaac Williams between 1846 and 1852.

September

- U.S. Commodore Robert F. Stockton and U.S. Lieutenant Archibald Gillespie are in Los Angeles.
- Americans begin taking Californios prisoner in Southern California.
- A group of Californios attack Gillespie's garrison. Gillespie's response to the attack is to install additional restrictions and curfews on Los Angeles.
- Battle of Chino, a skirmish occurs between Californios and American sympathizers at Isaac Williams' ranch house. Californio José del Carmen Lugo fights against his brother-in-law Isaac Williams and apprehends him and the other Americans at the ranch. Lugo's party commandeers the American's weapon supplies.
- Gillespie surrenders Los Angeles and is told to leave. Reinforcements arrive from San Francisco.

1846 *cont.*

- U.S. General Stephen Watts Kearny and 300 of the 1st Dragoons leave for California from Santa Fe, New Mexico.

October

- October 6, Kearny and his men meet with Kit Carson. Kearny receives news that California has been won. He sends 200 of his men back to Santa Fe and continues into California with Carson acting as his guide.
- October 8, Battle of the Old Woman's Gun (Battle of Dominguez Rancho).
- Lugo arrives in Temecula, hears word that the Indians in San Bernardino "had risen and were coming to commit outrages on the ranchos." He returns to San Bernardino to diffuse the situation.
- Lugo leaves San Bernardino and goes to Warner's Ranch in pursuit of Segura, a Californio who has taken defense funds from Los Angeles and seeks to flee the country.
- Lugo heads to Santa Ysabel in pursuit of Segura and encounters a group of Sonorans fleeing Sonora with a herd of horses. While camped at Santa Ysabel, the local Indian Capitan Mateo warns Lugo that the Indians from Pauma, Temecula, and Agua Caliente (Warner Springs) plan to attack during the night. The Californios send for reinforcements from San Diego. No attack occurs.

1846 ***cont.***

- Lugo goes to Pauma with Captain José Alipaz. He tasks Alipaz with escorting the Sonorans to San Luis Rey. Lugo then returns to Los Angeles via Pala and Temecula, San Bernardino.

NOVEMBER

- At Warner's Ranch, an American patrol arrests Jonathan Trumbull Warner, believing he is not loyal to the United States.

DECEMBER

- December 2, Kearny's 'Army of the West' arrives at Warner's Ranch. Kearny talks with the Indians at Agua Caliente.
- U.S. Lieutenant Davidson and Kit Carson raid a herd of horses and mules at Aguanga belonging to Mexican General José María Flores.
- Lugo enlists more men in San Bernardino and San Jacinto.
- December 4, Kearny and his men leave Warner's Ranch for San Diego.
- December 5, Kearny and his men meet with Lieutenant Archibald Gillespie who informs Kearny that General Andrés Pico is encamped at the San Pasqual village with a force of insurgents.
- December 6 and 7, Battle of San Pasqual.
- Sometime between December 8 and December 12 (likely dates), the Pauma Massacre occurs.

1847
- Late December and early January (exact dates are not known), The Temecula Massacre
- January 1, Full moon.
- January 13, Treaty of Cahuenga is signed resulting in cease fire between Californios and Americans.
- January 21, Mormon Battalion arrives at Warner's Ranch.
- January 24, A storm passes through, flooding the river and stalling the Battalion's march.
- January 25, Mormon Battalion reaches Temecula.
- January 26, "This morning the Indians were burying their dead." –Henry Standage, Mormon Battalion.
- January 31, Full moon.

1848
- February 2, Treaty of Guadalupe Hidalgo is signed between Mexico and the United States.
- July, Senator Thomas Hart Benton testifies to Congress against giving Kearny a "brevet," or an honorary promotion of rank, for his actions at the Battle of San Pasqual.
- July, The promotion by brevet of Stephen Watts Kearny is approved by a vote of 32 to 14 in the Senate.

1850 September 9, California becomes the 31st state of the United States of America.

1867
- May, The San Bernardino *Guardian* reports the Temecula locals are seeking funds to enclose the graveyard with "a neat and substantial fence."
- June 15, An unnamed priest wrote to Bishop Amat of the Los Angeles Diocese describing the graveyard and asking for permission to consecrate the cemetery.

1875 September 26-28, The Temecula Indians are evicted from their village and forced to move from the Temecula, Little Temecula, and Pauba Ranchos.

1877 October 30, Thomas Savage interviews 64-year-old José del Carmen Lugo for use as source material in Hubert Howe Bancroft's *History of California*.

1879 Birth of Antonio "Tony" Ashman, Pechanga Tribal elder interviewed by several historians about Tribal history. Ashman was born at a time of uncertainty for the Indian people, after the Temecula eviction but before the Pechanga Reservation was created.

1880 October 1, Alfred Perry Walbridge passes through Temecula, describing the cemetery as having only a few old adobe walls standing, and reports that the grave markers are aligned to the north.

1882
- George Cuishman dies and is buried at the Temecula Indian Cemetery. His headstone is the last remaining marker in the cemetery.
- June 28, Pechanga Indian Reservation is established by Executive Order.

1884 Helen Hunt Jackson's novel *Ramona* is published. The Temecula Eviction is depicted in the story.

1912 The Native Sons of the Golden West fraternity donate the site of the Battle of San Pasqual to the State of California.

1932-33 John P. Harrington interviews numerous Tribal people from several Southern California reservations. Information about the Temecula Massacre and Juan Antonio's role is recorded.

1937 August 10, John Harrington conducts an oral history interview with Pechanga Tribal Member Sargento Rodriguez, a Temecula Indian who survived the Massacre. He indicates a hundred men were killed and that the "coyotes ate the bones of the people."

1947 June 28, B.E. McCown leads an archaeological field survey of the Temecula River and adjacent areas to be flooded and disturbed by construction of the Vail Lake Dam. Seventeen sites are identified.

1948 Construction of Vail Lake Dam is completed.

1954 The San Pasqual Battlefield is designated a California Historical Landmark.

1969 Heavy rains flood the area, and the Vail Lake dam spillway is compromised and subsequently rebuilt.

1971 Horace Parker publishes *The Historic Valley of Temecula: The Temecula Massacre*, a culmination of his research from the 1950s and 1960s, which included interviews with Pechanga Tribal Member Antonio Ashman.

1991 Jack Roripaugh catches a group attempting to steal the Cuishman headstone and orders it returned.

1996 The Cuishman headstone is stolen again, but later returned to Pechanga.

2005 The area surrounding the Temecula Indian Cemetery is paved and developed for commercial use. The City of Temecula deeds the cemetery parcel to the Pechanga Band of Indians.

GLOSSARY

The following are 'Atáaxum (Luiseño) names and words. The pronunciation provided uses English phonetics.

Aguanga: [agh-WONGA] A village name that was derived from the 'Atáaxum (Luiseño) word, 'awáa, meaning dog; place of the dogs.

Apis: [AH-pish] A surname, the name of traditional clan.

'Atáaxum: [ah-TAAX-hum] An Indigenous person. This term is generally used to refer to oneself or others within the collective Native community. This can also refer to people from other Tribes, but generally used to refer to people who speak the same language (Luiseño).

Cahuilla: [Kah-WE-yah] The Tribe east of the 'Atáaxum (Luiseño).

Calac: [cah-LACK] A surname, name of a traditional clan.

'Éxva Teméeku: [EHK-va Teh-MEH-coo] Where the World was created, according to the 'Atáaxum (Luiseño) oral tradition, and from which the name of the City of Temecula is derived. The name comes from 'éxla, which means the earth, the land, and Temét, the Sun, thus creating the place name where the heavens and earth came together to form the World.

'Éxla: [EHK-la] The earth, dirt, soil.

'Éxval: [EHK-vaul] Sand.

Káamalam: [KAH-mah-lam] The First People to be born into the World from the union of Túukumit (Father Night Sky) and Tamáayawut (Mother Day Earth). This refers to all things in the World including mountains, rocks, plants, and animals.

Káamalam Pomkí: [KAH-mah-lam Pom-KEY] The house of the Káamalam, located on Pu'éska Mountain.

Móyla: [MOY-la] The Moon. Also known as the reincarnated Wuyóot who returned as the Moon three days after his death to continue to be with the Káamalam.

Páa'ila: [PAH-ela] Pond turtle. Also a Traditional clan name for a family from the Temecula Village, who still reside at Pechanga. Historically, the name was translated into Spanish, *Tortuga,* a name by which the family is also known.

Pauba: [PAUGH-ba] The name of the historic village where the Temecula people hid before the Temecula Massacre. The Mexican Rancho in which it was later located is also called by this name.

Pauma: [PAUGH-ma] The name of a historic village and the name of the reservation of the Pauma Band of Luiseño Indians. The Mexican Rancho of José Serrano was also called Pauma.

Pávkun: [PAHV-koon] The historic Temecula Cemetery where the Temecula Massacre victims are buried.

Pechanga: [peh-CHONG-ga] The name of the reservation established for the Native people evicted from their traditional village. This reservation is located adjacent to the City of Temecula's southern boundary. The Pechanga Reservation was established by Executive Order on June 27, 1882.

Pu'éska: [puh-ESKA] A sacred hill in Temecula. The name of the hill upon which the Creation of the World occurred and is the home of the Káamalam.

$óova: [SHOW-va]: The name of the village where the Mormon Battalion camped before reaching Temecula.

$úukat: [SHOE-cut] Deer. The first of the Káamalam to agree to become food after Wuyóot's death.

Tamáayawut: [tah-MY-ya-whoot] Mother Day Earth. She and Túukumit (Father Night Sky) created the World, as told in the 'Atáaxum (Luiseño) Creation account.

Temecula: [teh-MEH-que-la] A modern-day city in Southern California located about sixty miles north of San Diego. The name is derived from the 'Átáaxum (Luiseño) name 'Éxva Teméeku, the place where the Indigenous people of the region believe the World was created.

Temét: [teh-MET] The Sun. A Káamalam and key figure in the Creation of the World.

Tikithíkkish: [te-KEET-te-kish] The tradition of lighting candles at relatives' graves annually on November 2nd. The word means 'be continually lit.'

Tóovish: [TOH-vish] White clay. Tóovish was the first food of the Káamalam (First People), which was provided and prepared by Wuyóot.

Tótpa: [TOHT-pa] The name of a village located near Murrieta Hot Springs. Tótpa means place of rocks and water.

Túukumit: [TOO-koo-mit] Father Night Sky. He and Tamáayawut (Mother Day Earth) created the World, as told in the 'Atáaxum (Luiseño) Creation account.

Waxáawut: [wah-HOW-woot] Bullfrog. Also, the name for Frog Woman, the Káamalam who poisoned Wuyóot, causing his death.

Waxáwmay [wah-HOW-my] place anime meaning 'place of the frogs.' Birthplace of Pablo Apis, grantee of the Little Temecula Rancho, which encompasses the Temecula Village.

Wuyóot: [we-YOHT] The last of the Káamalam (First People) to be born and innately gifted with wisdom. He instructed the Káamalam on social organization and religious practices. His death was the first to occur in the World, introducing the practice of death rites and observances.

THE TEMECULA MASSACRE

OVERVIEW

THE 1846 TEMECULA MASSACRE IS AMONG the deadliest conflicts tied to the Mexican-American War. The sequence of events surrounding the Temecula Massacre illustrates a complex narrative of pre-statehood California. The Battle of San Pasqual is considered in the textbooks of United States and California history to be the bloodiest conflict of the War, with eighteen Americans killed. However, the loss of Native American lives during the Temecula Massacre, which occurred a few weeks after this battle, claimed four times that number. Further, in the aftermath, the bodies of the deceased were removed from where they were slaughtered and buried in a mass grave. The event and its people have since been overlooked in California annals.

According to the oral tradition of the 'Atáaxum—the Native people of the region—the World was created at 'Éxva Teméeku, in the valley now known as Temecula. The 'Atáaxum (also referred to in historical documents and published accounts as the Luiseño) believe the Káamalam (First People), were birthed in this valley, living here since time-immemorial. Knowledge of the Creation and the societal rules established by the First People were passed down for millennia.[1]

1 The 'Atáaxum/Luiseño Creation account was recorded several times by anthropologists and published in books and journal articles. The account is told through hundreds of traditional songs which are still sung today. The version shared here is greatly abbreviated and only includes the key points of a very complex and multifaceted Origin account.

Figure 1. 'Éxva Teméeku, the place of Creation. Photo by Myra Masiel-Zamora.

The 'Atáaxum Origin account tells of the creation of the World and the birth of the First People, the Káamalam, at 'Éxva Teméeku, near present day Temecula, California. The ancestral songs say Túukumit (Father Night Sky) and Tamáayawut (Mother Day Earth) created the World. Túukumit gave Tamáayawut the Sun, Temét as a gift which was cast into the sky with a special net made for this purpose.[2] When Túukumit and Tamáayawut became one, their first offspring called the Káamalam, were earth, 'éxla and sand, 'éxval, followed by all things, including mammals, birds, trees, fog, rocks, and people.

The last of the Káamalam born was Wuyóot. He was innately gifted with knowledge and knew how to make the first food, white clay called tóovish, to feed the Káamalam. He was much loved by the First People, and they lived for a long time in harmony, but one day he angered Waxáawut, Frog Woman, and she poisoned him. In an attempt to be cured, Wuyóot visited many hot springs throughout the traditional Tribal territory, and the First People accompanied him on this journey. As they traveled, he named several places along the way and counted the increments of time, which became known as the months of the year. As they traveled, Wuyóot taught the First People his knowledge, including societal rules, religious practices, and the ceremonial songs, which are still sung today.

Ultimately, Wuyóot could not be cured and upon his death his body was taken back to 'Éxva Teméeku, the birthplace of the World, and cremated. Wuyóot's passing was the first death known to the Káamalam and the traditional Tribal funeral observances and rites originated at this time. Since death was a new experience, the Káamalam were so overcome with grief that the quail, roadrunner, and woodpecker cut their hair, which is a mourning custom still practiced today.[3] The rocks cried, which still manifests on the rocks on Pu'éska Mountain, the location of 'Éxva Teméeku. Wuyóot's death frightened the people, but he told the Káamalam he would be resurrected as Móyla, the moon, in three days, before that event night had only been full of darkness. From that time on the Káamalam knew

2 William Duncan Strong, *Aboriginal Society in Southern California*, University of California Press. 1929, p. 295.

3 Philip Stedman Sparkman, 1908, The Culture of the Luiseño Indians, University of California Publications in American Archaeology and Ethnology, Vol. 8(4):187-234.

Figure 2. View of Temecula Massacre Battlefield Area, at present-day Vail Lake. Vail Lake Dam to left. Pechanga Cultural Resources Department 2019.

Móyla-Wuyóot would always be with them. After Wuyóot's death, the First People called a Grand Council at Káamalam Pomkí (First People's house), located in the hills above 'Éxva Teméeku. During this Council the Káamalam discussed who would become food, since tóovish (white clay) would no longer be provided by Wuyóot. After several arguments as to why certain Káamalam should not become food, it was determined that $úukat (deer) along with other plants and animals, would be sacrificed to sustain the people. Once the new order of the world was decided, the First People dispersed out to all corners of Creation, some became stars, others became the creatures that burrow into the ground, and many were the human people who settled in the Temecula Valley.

For the 'Atáaxum, upon death the soul travels to all points of creation, the cardinal directions, with the West—the Pacific Ocean and the southern Channel Islands—as the final destination before ascension into the sky. The Creation account is told through the translation of traditional song texts, which communicate the ceremonial practices, and social customs and traditions that were derived directly from Wuyóot and the creation of the Tribal world. The death rites are one of the most important observances for the 'Atáaxum and due to

the chaos and political unrest during this time it is unknown if the people slain during the Temecula Massacre were properly cared for in a ceremonial manner.

Long before Mexican occupation, the Native people of the region lived in large villages consisting of 50-200 people. Villages were comprised of family units, known as clans, each of which had their own leaders, advisors, and healers. Village populations interacted with neighboring groups, forming ties through intermarriage, trade, and ceremonial practices. The efficiency of traditional social organization amongst the Tribes of Southern California was noted by the first Spaniards to visit the area, including Father Junípero Serra who wrote in his diaries that he found the people of Alta California to be amiable and generous.[4]

When Spanish missionaries arrived in Southern California in 1769, the Native people came under the control of each local mission as it was established. The people became affiliated with each mission by name. The 'Atáaxam became known by the name "Luiseño" as their villages were under the influence of Mission San Luis Rey.

4 Rose Marie Beebe and Robert Senkewicz, 2013. "On the Road to San Diego: Junípero Serra's Baja California Diary." *Journal of San Diego History*, 59(4):180-240.

After the missions were secularized in 1834, the Native people were subjected to oppression and displacement under Mexican rule. In order to remain on their traditional homelands, the people had to work as laborers on the Mexican ranchos. It was during this era that the United States declared war on Mexico, forcibly and unavoidably including Native people in the fight for California's secession to the United States.

The Temecula Massacre was a proxy battle waged by a contingency of the Cahuilla, a neighboring Tribe, who aligned with the Mexican Californians to retaliate against the Luiseño for the murders of Californio leaders. The "Californios" were the wealthy families that had received large land grants from Spain and Mexico and prospered from California's agricultural resources during the 1830s and onward. As many as 100 Luiseño/Temecula Indians were killed in the ambush attack, which was the result of events associated with the Battle of San Pasqual and the Pauma Massacre. These events demonstrate the region's complex cultural climate and the impetus for the conquest of California by the Americans.

For the Pechanga Band of Indians, the descendants of the people who survived the massacre, the significance of these events became critical factors in the Tribe's future social and political path. Today, the Temecula Indian Cemetery is one of the last visages of the disastrous tumult of 1846-1847 and is a case study of contemporary historic preservation efforts. It stands inside an irreplaceable landscape with dynamic histories that demonstrate the cultural complexities of Native California. The cemetery also brings a paramount sense of place to the earliest known people and their descendants. These are living landscapes with stories that continue to be told, which possess continued significance. Often the experiences of Native people are lost through history, and only by unraveling the many perspectives of the Temecula Massacre can this pivotal intersection of California and Tribal histories begin to be understood.

MEXICAN-AMERICAN CONFLICTS, 1821-1846

In 1821, Mexico achieved independence from Spain, which for over two hundred years had established missions and presidios in what was known as New Spain since the sixteenth century. Unlike under Spanish rule, Mexican policies encouraged governors to award more land grants for individual *ranchos*, or large-tract, family-managed farms. As opposed to the Spanish period in Alta California (1769-1821) when only thirty rancho grants were authorized, over 800 grants were awarded during the Mexican period. In addition to land grants, one of the most significant changes under the new Mexican republic was to "secularize" the missions and remove the Natives and the mission's property from the control of the Catholic Church.

The California missions were already in decline by the 1820s, and the system itself was entirely dismantled by the Mexican government in 1834. This action effectively ended one chapter of cruelty and atrocity endured by California's Native people and ushered in a new period of challenges. Mexico ordered the Franciscans to give up control over the neophytes (mission subjects). Priests' authorities were reduced to the equivalent of parish priests, with little power over the people who lived in the region around the missions. Ex-neophytes were to be granted small tracts of land near the mission to form towns, or pueblos. However, most people moved inland away from the influence of the missions, rather than stay to work for the priests as wage labors.[5]

With few exceptions, most of the mission's land holdings were redistributed to Mexican citizens, and this emerging class bolstered their personal wealth by profiting off the mission-established enterprises and Native American labor. The secularization of the missions changed not only California Indians' place in society, but also the entire social structure. Mexico secularized the missions for several reasons. The system was seen to have ultimately failed in its efforts to assimilate the Indians and to subdue interior Tribes. Mexican citizens also wanted the land, livestock, and wealth the mission system had cultivated. Secularization similarly affected the Indian neophytes: few received mission lands, and many were displaced and became wage laborers or were conscripted for forced labor on the ranchos. Native people wishing to return to their villages now found themselves on lands owned by the Californios, which thrust them into a type of serfdom. The people could no longer rely solely on traditional foods and resources. Some provisions were needed such as beef, cloth, and food crops due to decades of destruction of the landscape by mission livestock grazing native grasslands as well as the creation of agricultural fields which altered natural creek runoff patterns and drove away deer and other animals.[6]

During the same years, Americans who had recently arrived in California saw an opportunity to amass wealth. Following the decline of the missions, cattle became the principal economy in California. Americans quickly became the principal trading partners in the

5 Robert H. Jackson and Edward Castillo, *Indians, Franciscans, and Spanish Colonization: The Impact of the Mission System on California Indians.* University of New Mexico Press, Albuquerque, 1995, pp. 90-97.

6 Virginia S. Popper, Change and Persistence: Mission Neophyte Foodways at Selected Colonial Alta California Institutions, *Journal of California and Great Basin Anthropology* Vol. 36, No. 1, 2016, pp. 5-25.

region. Commodities such as manufactured goods and Asian luxuries were traded for the hides and tallow of the vast cattle herds of the ranchos; these raw materials were soon supplying the shoe and soap industries of New England, while Californians became dependent on American products.[7] Historian George William Beattie, who studied the history of Southern California during this period, notes that all the while, Californios were well aware of the prosperity that had come to these outsiders, and were more or less resentful of it.[8]

One such American entrepreneur was Jonathan Trumbull Warner (also known as Juan José Warner). He left Connecticut in 1830, worked on wagon train companies in the Midwest, reaching California in 1837. While working in Los Angeles, Warner befriended well-known ranchero Pío Pico. Warner returned to the United States in 1839 to promote the West and offer lectures, wherein he stressed the significance of the Pacific Coast in the future development of the United States. Pennsylvanian Isaac Williams was another American who came to Southern California during the Mexican period and became one of the region's prominent *extranjeros* (foreigners). In 1835, Williams participated in the removal of Native people who resided on San Nicolas Island, one of the southern Channel Islands off the coast of California, taking a young woman to live with him.[9] She died shortly after she was baptized as María Magdalena in 1836.

In 1839, Williams married thirteen-year-old María Lugo, the daughter of prominent Californio Don Antonio María Lugo—known as "El Viejo" due to his position as the patriarch of his large family. El Viejo was one of the largest landowners in Alta California. At that time, to marry a daughter of one of these landowners was seen in some respects as a quicker way to clean her family of it its assets than

7 Robert V. Hine and John Mack Faragher, *Frontiers: A Short History of the American West*, Yale University Press: New Haven, 2007.

8 Beattie, George William, "The Battle of Chino." *The Quarterly: Historical Society of Southern California* 24 (4): 1942, pp. 143-160.

9 William Henry Ellison, *The Life and Adventures of George Nidever 1802-1883*. McNally & Loftin, Publishers, Santa Barbara. 1984, p. 37.

to lend money to the "old man Lugo."[10] Williams acquired the Santa Ana del Chino rancho from El Viejo in 1841; the prosperous ranch would later become a station along the Butterfield stage route. María Lugo had three children by Williams but died in childbirth in 1842. Of María Lugo's children, her son died young, but the two daughters went on to have little association with their uncle, José del Carmen Lugo, the orchestrator of the Battle of Chino and the Temecula Massacre. Lugo lamented in his late years, that the girls "cared nothing about their uncle."[11]

During the Mexican period, San Luis Rey Mission mayordomo (manager) Pablo Apis, Sr., received one of the very few land grants awarded to California Indians. Apis, born circa 1792 at the village of Waxáwmay (Rancho Guajome) near the mission, was educated by the priests. In 1845, Governor Pio Pico granted Apis, the "Little Temecula Rancho," consisting of a half-league of land (about 2,200 acres) in the Temecula Valley as a reward for his service to the Mission. The Temecula Indian village, which predated the mission era and had a population of over two hundred, was located within this grant.[12] Even though, Apis owned the land and oversaw the management and operations of the Rancho, he was not the leader of the Village, the Tribal people retained their traditional hereditary leadership customs and governing practices. Apis later aligned himself with the Californios at the Battle of San Pasqual, thus pledging his allegiance to Mexico, while several of the men of the Temecula Village favored the Americans.[13]

---

10 Bell, Horace, *Reminiscences of a Ranger: Early Times in Southern California.* University of Oklahoma Press 1999, pp. 174-176.

11 Beattie, Helen Pruitt, English translation of *Life of a Rancher* by Don José Carmen Lugo, Los Angeles, 1877, and Interview conducted by Thomas Savage collected for use as source material in Hubert Howe Bancroft's *History of California.* 1950, p. 13.

12 Leland E. Bibb, Leland E., "Pablo Apis and Temecula," The Journal of San Diego History, San Diego Historical Society Quarterly, Fall 1991, Volume 37, Number 4.

13 Woodward, Arthur, Lances at San Pascual. California Historical Society: San Francisco, 1948, Appendix E, p. 65.

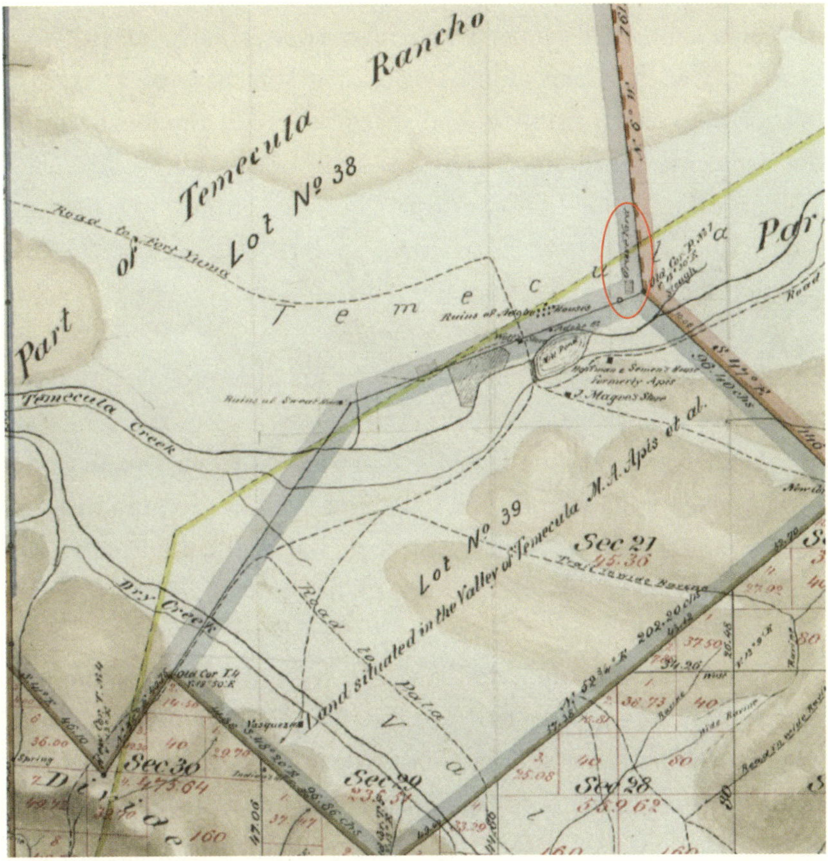

Figure 3. Excerpt of the 1880 plat map depicting the junction of three rancho boundaries, the Temecula, Little Temecula, and the Pauba Ranchos. Note the Temecula Massacre Cemetery is depicted in the red oval, labeled "Graveyard."

Isaac Williams' relationship with the Apis family began in 1844-1845 when Williams brokered a deal to secure Native American labor for his cattle enterprise. In 1846, Williams established relationships with two young Luiseño cousins, María Antonia Apis and María de Jesusa Apis. The girls, ages thirteen or fourteen, each bore a daughter to Isaac Williams, who was forty-seven at the time. María Antonia

Apis had four children by Williams between 1846 and 1852.[14] It is speculated that this unusual situation was part of a "patron" relationship, which firmly bound the Apis family, the Luiseño, and the Temecula Village to the Williams family at Chino.[15] Although Williams died in 1856, this relationship was continued by his son-in-law, John Rains, until he too died, in 1862 clearly exploiting the practice of usurping land from the Indians.[16]

California was a distant province that Mexico proved to have difficulty ruling. When the Mexican government appointed Manuel Micheltorena governor of the province in 1842, he was not popular amongst the local citizenry and a revolt began against him. Micheltorena resigned in 1845, and Pío Pico became the civil governor, based at Los Angeles. In many ways, all but officially, Alta California achieved some measure of independence from Mexico during this time.

Meanwhile, the Luiseño bands that lived around Temecula, Palomar Mountain, Pala, and San Pasqual had a population of over 2,000, with numerous villages varying in size located along the main roads. California was not an empty expanse only to be populated by mostly white Americans heading west following the discovery of gold in 1849, as it is portrayed in many accounts of the region. To the contrary, a significant population of both Tribal people and Californios were long established there and had built well-constructed trails and fostered extensive trade networks. The range of the trail connections to villages and communities are illustrated through numerous diaries, oral accounts, and maps that demonstrate the ease with which the Native Americans and later Californios were able to navigate the region.

14 Anne J. Miller, 2004. María Antonia Apis: A Young Luiseño Indian Woman. *Southern California Quarterly* Vol. 86, No.2, pp. 113-126, 119.

15 Bibb, 1991.

16 Ibid.

DECLARATION OF WAR

TWENTY-TWO YEARS AFTER MEXICO ACHIEVED ITS independence from Spain, the United States declared war on Mexico. The Mexican-American War largely emerged from Americans' eagerness to expand westward to the Pacific Ocean; as many American settlers ventured west, they began to resent the fact that the lands to the south and west of the Louisiana Purchase tract remained territories of Mexico.[17] Upon taking office, President James K. Polk prioritized the acquisition of Mexico's northern territories; however, his proposals were rebuked and sparked a wave of indignation and nationalist fervor in Mexico.[18] Polk sent the first U.S. troops to the Rio Grande River in January of 1846.

Figure 4. US General Stephen Watts Kearny, engraving by T.B. Welch (Courtesy of Library of Congress. Prints and Photographs Division, LC-USZ62-17905.)

17 Harlow, Neal, *California Conquered: The Annexation of a Mexican Province 1846-1850*. University of California Press, Berkeley, 1982, p. 4.

18 Walker, Dale L., *Bear Flag Rising: The Conquest of California, 1846*. Tom Doherty Associates, 1999, pp. 59-68 and Harlow, 1982, pp. 52-58.

The war resulted in a swift change in the society and culture of the entire Southern California region, especially in denser population centers, like San Diego and Los Angeles. It also created political divisions between the Californios and the newly settled Americans who were enmeshed with the Mexican-Californio elite. And it provided cause for further hostilities between the Californios and the Native people, who after several decades became accustomed to Mexican rule and societal norms. The Americans brought a new mindset and governing approach which appeared superior and more progressive than the localized governing practices of Mexico.

By the eve of the Mexican-American War, the Temecula Indians had forged significant connections with some of the Americans newly living in California, and by the fall of 1846, they were deeply embroiled in the fight and aligned themselves with the United States.

In late September 1846, U.S. General Stephen Watts Kearny left Santa Fe, New Mexico with his Army of the West, comprised of 300 men of the 1st Dragoons, Companies C and K en route to California. When they left, Colonel Philip St. George Cooke, an officer in Kearny's Dragoons, was tasked to recruit an army in Iowa that would later follow them to California. The troop Cooke assembled became known as the Mormon Battalion. Upon Kearny's departure, Cooke noted that "tomorrow three hundred wilderness-worn dragoons, in shabby and patched clothing, who have long been on short allowance of food, set forth to conquer or 'annex' a Pacific empire."[19] In short, their mission was to assist in the conquest of California for the United States.

19 Cooke, Captain Phillip St. George, *The Conquest of New Mexico and California in 1846-1848,* Chicago: Rio Grande Press. 1878. The army that Cooke assembled in Council Bluffs, Iowa was the Mormon Battalion.

Figure 5. "Kearny's Army Crossing the Great Plains—1846" by K. M. Chapman in *The History of the Military Occupation of New Mexico* by Ralph Emerson Twitchell, 1909, pg. 29.

On October 6th, Kearny and his men met with Christopher Houston "Kit" Carson, a well-known frontiersman, who was carrying a message to Washington announcing (prematurely, as it turned out) the conquest of California, and that the American Flag was flying from every important position in the territory.[20] Kearny, then under the impression that Lieutenant Colonel John C. Frémont and Commodore Robert F. Stockton had already secured the region, sent 200 of his men back to Santa Fe and pressed on with a smaller party into California with Carson acting as his guide.[21] Carson had recently gar-

20 Frémont, John Charles, *Memoirs of My Life*. Chicago: Belford, Clarke & Co. 1887, p. 585.

21 Commodore Robert F. Stockton was given the temporary title of commodore in 1846, promoted from the rank of captain. By 1850, Stockton returned to his rank of captain. President Polk promoted Lieutenant Colonel John C. Frémont to his position in June 1846. At this point in time, in the hierarchy of rank, the reporting order would have filtered down from Commodore Stockton to General Kearny, and then to Lieutenant Colonel Frémont.

nered a commission as a lieutenant of the United States Mounted Volunteers, so he had no recourse when Kearny ordered him, despite his objection, to reverse his course and join Kearny's troops to serve as a guide on the trail.[22]

Kit Carson began his career in the West by escorting caravans to New Mexico, as a mountain man and fur trapper. It was his experience as a guide during the 1842 Frémont expeditions that propelled him into fame. During the 1860s, the federal government would commission him to lead a campaign to eradicate the Navajo and Apache, in a brutal attempt to subdue and exile the Tribes. It was in New Mexico in 1864 when Carson exacted his scorched earth policy for the Navajo homeland, destroying everything in his path. Some 8,000 Navajo were forced to march 400 miles through the desert, known as the "Long Walk" to Fort Sumner in Bosque Redondo, New Mexico Territory.[23]

Figure 6. Kit Carson, photograph taken between 1860 and 1875. (Courtesy of Library of Congress, Prints & Photographs Division, Brady-Handy photograph collection, LC-DIG-cwpbh-00514.)

On December 2, 1846, Kearny's 'Army of the West' arrived at Warner's Ranch weary and exhausted from their 2,000-mile journey through the desert. Only a few weeks prior, a United States reconnaissance patrol visited Warner's Ranch and arrested the ranch's owner, Jonathan Trumbull Warner, when it was suspected he

22 Hollon, Cory S. "'A Leap in the Dark': The Campaign to Conquer New Mexico and California, 1846–1847," *Army History*, Winter 2015, No. 94, p.18.

23 Bailey, Lynn Robinson, Bosque Redondo: An American concentration Camp, Socio-Technical Books, Pasadena, 1970.

Figure 7. Contextual view of Warner's Ranch. The ranch house is in the center and trading post/barn is on right. Note approximate locations of Overland Trail (now paved highway) in front of house. (Courtesy of Library of Congress, Prints and Photographs Division, HABS, Reproduction number CAL,37-WARN.V,1-4.)

was not loyal to the United States.[24] Warner was granted the property from the Mexican governor Pío Pico earlier that same year. When the Mormon Battalion arrived at Warner's Ranch in January 1847, Cooke described Warner as "quite a study"; a Connecticut man-turned California proprietor who exhibited the traits of either character.[25]

At the time of the army's arrival, the ranch's caretaker, a Rhode Island emigrant named William Marshall, greeted Kearny and his men instead. Marshall provided what information he had on California affairs but was quickly determined to be of little use to

24 Bibb, Leland E., "William Marshall: 'The Wickedest Man in California,'" *The Journal of San Diego History, San Diego Historical Society Quarterly,* Winter 1976, Vol. 22, No. 1.

25 Cooke, Phillip St. George, *Report from the Secretary of War, communicating, in compliance with a resolution of the Senate, of the 21st February, 1849, a copy of the official journal of Lieutenant Colonel Philip St. George Cooke, from Santa Fe to San Diego,* United States Congress Senate, p. 80.

the military campaign and intelligence.[26] While at Warner's Ranch, Kearny also encountered California Indians from various Tribes, and it is speculated that during these interactions it was made known that the Temecula Indians favored the American cause.

Meanwhile, Californio leader, Antonio Coronel, sent an Indian messenger to warn the Californio troops nearby at San Pasqual Village that the Americans were on the approach. Californio General Andrés Pico reportedly did not believe this message. His lack of confidence later perhaps resulted in the unpreparedness of his men when the Americans attacked.[27]

Kearny and his men left Warner's Ranch on December fourth for San Diego, and the next day they met Lieutenant Archibald Gillespie and Lieutenant Edward F. Beale who were accompanied by twenty-six marines from San Diego. Gillespie informed Kearny that General Andrés Pico was encamped at the San Pasqual village with a force of insurgents. Kearny then sent a party of men to survey the area to confirm if these rumors were true; however, the operation was quickly discovered when a barking dog alerted the Californios to their presence.[28] The Californios troops, numbering about 150, prepared for battle.

26 Bibb 1976 and Cooke, 1849, p. 80.

27 Dunn, Dana Ruth Hicks, *Strategies for Survival: Indian Transitions in the Mountains of San Diego County, 1846-1907.* University of California, Riverside Theses and Dissertations. 2013, p. 5.

28 Woodward, Arthur, "Lances at San Pasqual," *California Historical Society Quarterly*, Vol. 26, No. 1, March 1947, pp. 21-62.

THE BATTLE OF SAN PASQUAL

THE BATTLE OF SAN PASQUAL, FOUGHT between Kearny's men and the Californios, occurred on December 6 and 7, 1846. Pico's troops, who were ostensibly outnumbered and fighting with lances, swords, and flintlock muskets, pretended to retreat. The Americans were thus shocked when the Californios turned to confront them. Some of the men attempted to fire their weapons, only to discover their powder was so damp it would not ignite. The wet weather of previous days had rendered the army's carbines nearly useless.[29] The soldiers resorted to using their sabers and rifle butts to defend themselves; these weapons, however, proved to be no match for the horse-mounted Californios' long lances. This tactic was such a surprise to Kearny's troops that they were forced to take up a defensive position atop a nearby knoll. On December 7, the dragoons fought in a smaller skirmish against the Californios and suffered no casualties. Hoping to starve them into surrender, the Californio troops surrounded Kearny's force. While sequestered thusly on the hill, the men waited for help.

29 Hollon, 2015, p. 18.

Figure 8. Painting of the Battle of San Pasqual by Charles H. Waterhouse, 1979. Command Museum, Marine Corps Recruit Depot, San Diego.

A man from Temecula Village, José Páa'ila also known as José Tortuga [both surnames mean turtle] helped to save the Americans trapped on Mule Hill by cautiously slipping around the California patrols by traveling to San Diego to bring help. In the field notes of John P. Harrington, a linguist and ethnologist who recorded Southern California's Tribal languages and cultures during the twentieth century, recorded oral accounts of the battle. Harrington interviewed several people from the nearby reservations and a few of the consultants shared specific information that is not found in any other primary sources. One of Harrington's main Luiseño consultants, José Albañez from Potrero, referenced in the notes as "Joez," stated:

> Páa'ila was the name of a Temecula Indian who saved the [American] Soldiers that were cut off at vicinity of Hodges Lake. [Mexicans] on horseback were patrolling

> the place, when one [Mexican] mounted patrol stopped to take a smoke that broke the line, so the Indian who was lying there in the dark went through and went on foot to Old Town and the other American Soldiers came. Andres Tortuga, living at Pichanga [sic] now, is grandson of that Páa'ila.[30]

Frémont, in his 1887 memoirs, recalls the incident and points out that an Indian messenger (Tortuga) went into San Diego following the battle, leaving on the evening of the ninth with Kit Carson and Lieutenant Edward F. Beale, and that "the three had separated, taking different routes, in hope that at least one of them would reach the town. Living at San Diego, he [Tortuga] was familiar with the ground and was the first to get in."[31] The journey into San Diego was so difficult that Carson was "disabled for several days," and Beale reportedly took two years to recover from the injuries he sustained that night.[32] The monument in San Pasqual Battlefield State Historic Park, constructed in 1910, titled *Beale and Carson Hailing Stockton's Flagship,* depicts only Carson and Beale, omitting Tortuga's role in helping to save the Americans.

Once the Californio soldiers learned the Americans were alerted of the battle, most fled the San Pasqual Valley, returning to their homes and ranchos throughout Southern California. When the stand off was over both sides claimed victory. Kearny claimed a tactical victory because the Californios left the field first, even though he lost eighteen of his men, compared to Pico's loss of one man.[33] Furthermore, Pico maintained that he had never intended to fight the

30 *John Peabody Harrington Papers*, 1907-1959, Volume 3, Reel 116, Frame 217. Documents on file at Pechanga Cultural Resources department. The Luiseño word for turtle is Páa'ila, which is translated as Tortuga in Spanish.

31 Frémont, John Charles, *Memoirs of My Life*. Chicago: Belford, Clarke & Co. 1887, pp. 583-584.

32 Sabin, Edward Legrand, *Kit Carson Days, 1809-1868: Adventures in the Path of Empire,* Volume 2. University of Nebraska Press: Lincoln, reprint 1995.

33 Hallaran, 1991, p. 3.

Americans; rather, his only concern was to escape from his pursuers. Pico did also state that he "could not resist the temptation" to attack the Americans because their pursuit was so disorderly and their appearance, on mules, aroused the contempt of his followers, men born to the saddle.[34]

Modern-day Californians may know this battlefield site as the San Pasqual Valley, home to the San Diego Zoo Wildlife Park, south of the City of Escondido. "Mule Hill," as it has since been renamed, is in recognition of the place where the men took cover and resorted to eating their mounts and burning their equipment while waiting for rescue. In 1919, a plot of ground was donated to the State of California and in 1922 the Native Sons of the Golden West and the Daughters of the Revolution created markers with inscriptions with the names of the fallen American soldiers.[35] The park was designated a California Historical Landmark in 1954. The San Pasqual Battlefield State Historic Park spans fifty acres and is situated on land that was originally the

Figure 9. Monument located at San Pasqual Battlefield State Historic Park of Beale and Carson Hailing Stockton's Flagship, installed 1910. Pechanga Cultural Resources Department, 2018.

34 Regan, Geoffrey, *SNAFU: Great American Military Disasters*, Avon Books. 1993, p. 102.

35 Peet, Mary Rockwood, *San Pasqual: A Crack in the Hills*. The Highland Press, Culver City, 1949, 215-216.

San Pasqual Indian village. Living history demonstrations are performed annually at the park on the anniversary of the battle.

In August of 1847, following the close of the war, tensions between Stephen Watts Kearny and John C. Frémont came to fruition. Frémont was appointed governor of California by Commodore Robert F. Stockton, but Kearny never formally recognized his governorship, nor was it confirmed by the President or Secretary of War. Kearny ordered Frémont to surrender his position, to which Frémont complied; however, while traveling back to the U.S. with Kearny, he arrested Frémont for disobedience of orders.[36]

Frémont was court martialed in Washington, found guilty, and dismissed from service in the Army. However, President Polk quickly remitted the penalty and ordered Frémont to resume his sword and report for duty.[37] He did so, but shortly afterward he resigned his commission and left the Army.[38] Following the court martial in 1848, the legislature proposed to bestow Kearny with a brevet, or an honorary promotion of rank, for his actions at the Battle of San Pasqual.

Senator Thomas Hart Benton, who also happened to be Frémont's father-in-law, called into question the idea of honoring Kearny.[39] In Benton's testimony to Congress in July 1848, he called out three displays of misconduct on behalf of Kearny that could have precluded him from receiving laurels for his actions in California. First, Benton cited Kearny's behavior when his troops initially met with Kit Carson on their way into California in 1846. Benton stated that Kearny did not allow Carson to continue carrying the message from Commodore Robert F. Stockton that California had effectively already been won,

36 Guinn, James Miller, *A History of California and an Extended History of Los Angeles and Environs*, Historical Record Company: Los Angeles, California. 1915, p. 145.

37 Ibid.

38 Ibid.

39 Benton, Thomas Hart, "Nomination of General Kearny: Substance of the Speech of Mr. Benton, of Missouri, In the Senate—Executive Session," July 1848, from *The Congressional Globe for the First Session, Thirtieth Congress: Containing Speeches and Important State Papers*, Blair and Rives: Washington, p. 977.

that Lieutenant Colonel John C. Frémont was put in place as governor, and that the American flag was flying from every important post in the territory. Benton posited that this message should have continued to be carried on by the messenger himself, and that Kearny's order for Carson to return to California to guide his troops was a breach of protocol.

When Kit Carson was interviewed by Congress regarding this facet he stated:

> "I met General Kearny, with his troops, on the 6th of October…when I met them, the first thing I told them was that they were "too late"—that California was conquered, and the United States flag raised in all parts of the country. But General Kearny said he would go on; and said something about going to establish a civil government. I told him a civil government was already established, and Colonel Fremont appointed governor, to commence as soon as he returned from the north, some time in that very month (October). General Kearny said that was no difference; that he was a friend of Colonel Fremont, and he would make him governor himself. He began from the first to insist on my turning back to guide him into California. I told him I could not turn back—that I pledged myself to Commodore Stockton and Colonel Fremont to take their despatches [sic] through to Washington City, and to return with them as far as New Mexico, where my family lived, and to carry them all the way back if I did not find some one [sic] at Santa Fe that I could trust as well as I could myself; that I had promised them I would reach Washington in sixty days, and that they should have return despatches [sic] from the Government in one

hundred and twenty days."[40]

The second grievance Benton called out was that Kearny did not redirect his entire force upon hearing that California was secured. Although Kearny sent a large number of his soldiers back to New Mexico, he himself continued into California with a guard contingent. Benton suggested that Kearny was motivated by the desire to take the honors of California's conquest for himself and that he turned his back on the war that was raging in Mexico to do so.

Thirdly, Benton cited the Battle of San Pasqual itself, its sequence and humiliating defeat, as well as the possibility that Kearny might have falsified his accounts in order to aggrandize the event as a probable reason to court martial Kearny and withhold the proposed brevet.[41] Among the further discrepancies Benton pointed out, one challenged Kearny's account that he had acquired a large number of horses from a group of over-landers near Warner's Ranch; as when the battle occurred a few days later, his troops had but only a few tired mules.[42] To whom these horses went is unknown, but the value of this commodity at the time is significant.

Benton's personal relationship with Frémont undoubtedly shaded his opinion against Kearny, however many shared his view that the Battle of San Pasqual was to be regarded as a defeat and that Kearny did not deserve to be awarded a brevet. Ultimately, Benton's sharp commentary against Kearny failed. His attempt to appear unbiased and his testimony did not convince a majority in Congress. The promotion by brevet of Stephen Watts Kearny was approved by a vote of 32 to 14 in the Senate.[43] Furthermore, Kearny was given a promotion

40 Excerpted from Frémont, *Memoirs of My Life*. Chicago: Belford, Clarke & Co. 1887, pp. 585-586.
41 Benton, 1848, p. 977.
42 Benton, 1848, p. 1028.
43 United States Congress. Senate. *Journal of the Executive Proceedings of the Senate of the United States of America, From December 1, 1845, to August 14, 1848, Inclusive*. Vol. VII. Government Printing Office: Washington. 1887, pp. 473-474.

to major general for his "gallant and meritorious conduct in New Mexico and California, to date from the battle of San Pasqual."[44]

In 1923, Historian Orra Eugene Monnette described the Battle of San Pasqual as a "baptism by blood of the thought and principle of the advance, growth, and development of the American Nation."[45] Sentiments like these are echoed throughout romanticized accounts of the Battle of San Pasqual, which have pervaded the subject since.

Even though the skirmish occurred near the Indian village of San Pasqual, there is little historical information about the number of Native Americans involved in the Battle beyond Apis and Tortuga's roles. Apis, as a landowner, fought with the Californios to protect his rights; however, Tortuga's assistance with aiding the Americans trapped on the battlefield suggests an underlying sentiment amongst the Tribal communities that life would be better under the U.S. Government.

44 Ibid, p. 474.

45 Monnette, Orra Eugene, "Fort Moore and the Battle of San Pasqual." *Annual Publication of the Historical Society of Southern California*, Vol. 12, No. 3 (1923), p. 48.

THE PAUMA MASSACRE

After the Battle of San Pasqual, the Californio forces broke off into smaller groups and dispersed back to their homes and ranchos. The sudden appearance of Stockton's marines, who had come to rescue Kearny's forces gave the Californios such a shock that they were transformed from vigilant besiegers into panic-stricken fugitives.[46] The Indian women of the area were familiar with the abuses by foreign men, and immediately reacted to the arrival of the Californios by running away into the hills to hide.[47] This was common during the early periods of contact with the Spanish as it is documented that Spanish soldiers routinely raped and abused Indian women.[48] Some groups of Californios took to the hills and formed disorganized bands that stole horses and property. One of these groups, escorted by Pauma Rancho land grantee José Antonio Serrano, consisted of eleven of Pico's men. Pico was able to reorganize most of his forces and move on toward Los Angeles, while Serrano brought these eleven men to his ranch. While traveling to Serrano's adobe, they attacked and killed several Indians while stealing a herd of Luiseño horses and other property.[49]

---

46 Hudson, Millard, "The Pauma Massacre," *The Southern California Quarterly*, Vol. 7, Number 1, 1906, pp. 13-21.

47 Roberts, Elizabeth Judson, *Indian Stories of the Southwest*. San Francisco: Harr Wagner Publishing Co., 1917, pp. 221-222.

48 Dunn, 2013, p. 18.

49 Hayes, Benjamin, *Pioneer Notes from the Diaries of Judge Benjamin Hayes, 1849-1875*, Arno Press, New York, reprint 1976, p. 286.

The group included several members of his own family, his brother Manuel Serrano and their brother-in-law Ramón Aguilar from San Juan Capistrano. Also among them was Santos Alipás, Serrano's nephew, a fourteen-year-old boy who was sent from San Diego to carry provisions to his father. The rest of the group was comprised of: Sergeant Francisco Basualdo of San Diego whose wife was a cousin to the Governor Pico; Mariano Dominguez, also known as "Dominguito" from Los Angeles;[50] Santiago Osuna, a son of San Diego's well-known Dona Juliana Osuna; José Lopez and José María Alvarado from San Diego; Estaquio Ruiz, a relative of the Picos; and Juan de la Cruz and a New Mexican of unknown name, both of whom are described in various accounts as men who came from the North. This cadre of eleven men were eminent and highly positioned members of the Californio elite.

Figure 10: Juan Antonio Serrano. William Ellsworth Smythe's *History of San Diego 1542-1908*, The History Company, San Diego, 1908, page 175.

Although Serrano had received the Pauma land grant just two years prior, in 1844, he could trace his family's lineage in California back to the eighteenth century, when his grandfather came to San Diego with Father Junípero Serra. Juan Antonio's wife Rafaela, who he married in 1838, was the daughter of Rosario Aguilar the majordomo of the San Diego Mission.[51]

50 Hayes, 1976, p. 285.

51 Smythe, William Ellsworth, *History of San Diego, 1542-1908*. San Diego:History Co., 1907, p. 175.

The Pauma Rancho was located about a mile and a half from the Indian village at Pauma. The night of Serrano's group's arrival (likely between December 8th and December 12th), a contingent of Tribal men led by Manuelito Cota, the leader of all the Luiseño Bands, came to the adobe and apprehended the soldiers, brought them to Warner's Ranch where they were later executed after a meeting with other Tribal leaders.[52]

Upon hearing of the Californios capture, a group of Indians from a nearby village set out to secure their release but arrived too late.[53] This event became known as the Pauma Massacre, and worked to solidify Californio and Mexican fears that the Indians were being enticed by the Americans.

Accounts of the event suggest Serrano overheard two Luiseño women talking about a plot to capture the men. The fact that Indians vastly outnumbered Californios and Mexicans in 1846 had already created animosity and tension amongst the groups. Although the plot was made known to Serrano's guests, it appears no one took this threat seriously. Serrano's friendship with Manuelito Cota likely dissuaded any fears they may have had.

Dispute and uncertainty surround the actual date of the events and the motivation for the killings. During the early twentieth century, historian Millard F. Hudson interviewed surviving relatives of people associated with the Pauma Massacre. Hudson posits that their motivation stemmed from anger and resentment for the poor treatment the Indians endured from the Mexicans, and also because the people who stole their food and livestock went unpunished.[54] The victims of the Pauma Massacre were men of importance, some with familial connections to Governor Pío Pico, and others who were

52 Hayes, 1976, p. 285-286.

53 Phillips, George Harwood, *Chief and Challengers: Indian Resistance and Cooperation in Southern California, 1769-1906*. University of California Press, Berkeley, 1975, p. 49.

54 Hudson, 1907, pp. 14-17.

steeped in the Mexican-Californio elite and mission-era authorities. Therefore, another possible motivation for the massacre was that by targeting these high-profile men, a message was sent to Mexican forces that stealing from the Indians was unacceptable and justice would be carried out.

On the night of the execution, Cota took the captives from Serrano's adobe at Pauma and brought them to Cupa, the Indian village at Warner Springs, also known as Agua Caliente. Along the way, Cota first "exhibited the men to their neighbors and gave them an opportunity to participate in the ceremonies; and second, to hold a council as to what should be done with them."[55] Cota was in favor of setting the prisoners free, but was out-numbered. At Cupa, Luiseño and Cupeño leaders came together along with other leaders, including Cahuillas from Los Coyotes Village, to discuss what ramifications the prisoners would endure for stealing horses and killing Luiseño men; ultimately, the decision was to sentence them to death.[56]

It is important to note that this exercise in exacting justice was proffered to the American and Mexican public as a "massacre." As historian Horace Parker points out, "the killing of the Californians at the Agua Caliente on the Warner's ranch is now known as the Pauma Massacre. It seems to have been a frontier rule that when only whites were involved in a conflict it was called a battle; but when Indians were involved it became a massacre."[57] Cloaking the event as a massacre strips Native perspectives completely, divests tribal leadership of its enterprise and agency, and perpetuates derogatory narratives of Native people. Furthermore, the event merely began at Pauma, but culminated at the Indian village at Warner Springs. Therefore, calling the event the "Pauma Massacre" is a complete misnomer, and demeans the well-considered judgment and sentencing of a multi-tribal council,

55 Hudson, 1907, p. 18.

56 Dunn, 2013, pp. 27-28.

57 Parker, Horace, "The Temecula Massacre." *Westerners Brand Book* No. 10, pp. 176-188. Los Angeles: *Los Angeles Corral* No. 10, 1963, p. 10.

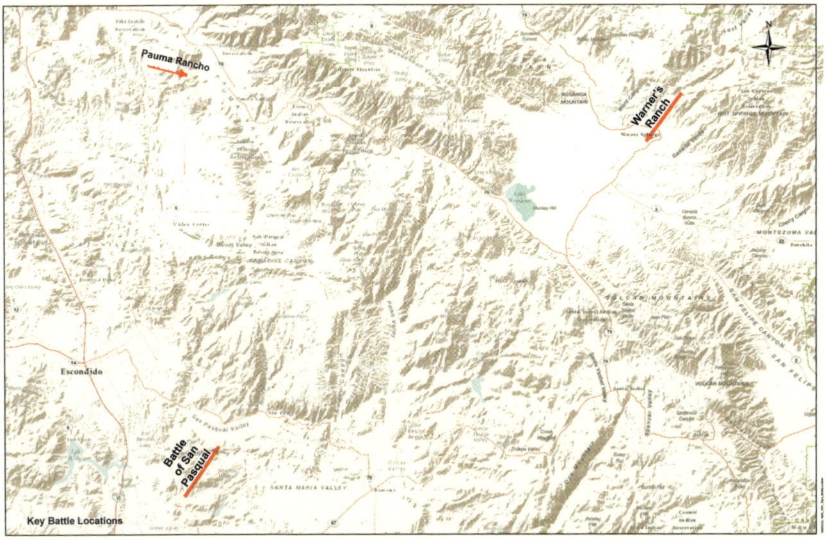

Figure 11: 1901 Topographic Map depicting the locations of the Battle of San Pasqual, Pauma Rancho, and Warner Springs (not to scale). USGS 1904.

an example of the chronic wrongdoing over time of American history accounting.

Upon hearing of the event, the Californio faction was further fueled with a desire to subdue the interior tribes. Sordid renditions of the ways the prisoners were executed also worked to spark the fervor of revenge. There are two prevailing versions of the execution: one describes the prisoners as made to stand and then shot with arrows, and another describes the prisoners as put to death by fire-heated lances. The youngest prisoner, fourteen-year-old Santo Alipas, was shot. Descriptions of the event report that the boy implored his fellow prisoners that they should die like brave men and not beg for their lives.

Dr. John S. Griffin, a physician to Kearny's forces, remarked:

> "A report reached our camp the other day that the Indians had killed eleven Mexicans, who had first attacked the Indians, killed five or six and taken their cattle and

> horses. At night the Indians surrounded the Mexican camp, captured the party, took them off to some distance, and shot them to death with arrows. All tell the same story as regards the number killed, but vary as to the manner. Those best versed in California affairs believe these men were killed in the action of the sixth, and that the Mexicans conceal their own loss by complaining of the redskins. They acknowledge one killed and 14 desperately wounded. After the action of San Bernardo (San Pascual) [sic] I sent word to Pico that I would be most happy to attend the wounded. He replied, he had none. It is now said his men are in the greatest state of excitement against him for not accepting my services."[58]

According to historian Richard Carrico, the Pauma Massacre was probably both an act of revenge and justice, and an assertion of power orchestrated by Cota to curry favor with the Americans and exhibit bravado.[59] There were attempts to link General Kearny with the Pauma Massacre, concerning advice he gave to representatives of the Indians at Santa Ysabel, when they expressed willingness to aid the American cause.[60] Kearny advised them to remain neutral, however Manuelito Cota insisted years later that Kearny also indicated that the Indians had a right to defend themselves from any acts on the part of the Mexicans.[61] When the Mormon Battalion came into California in 1847, their leadership made it known that they were not equipped or able to protect the Indians from Californio forces. Nonetheless, the deaths of the eleven men were interpreted as the result of a sinister

---

58 Hayes, 1976.

59 Carrico, Richard, *Strangers in a Stolen Land: Indians of San Diego County from Prehistory to the New Deal.* Sunbelt Publications, California. 2008, p. 45.

60 Hudson, 1906, p. 16.

61 Ibid.

Native attack based on an allegiance toward the American cause.

In 1878, William Marshall, the caretaker at Warner's Ranch who met Kearny's troops prior to the Battle of San Pasqual, was implicated in encouraging the Indians to kill the eleven prisoners. Californio Juana Machado Wrightington's claimed in her 1878 reminiscences that Marshall "was an instigator of the Pauma Massacre, for which crime he was hanged in '51."[62] From brief, confused statements, a large body of writings emerged during the twentieth century that portrayed Marshall as the "Wickedest Man in California."[63] However, primary sources fail to provide evidence of Marshall's participation. In actuality, Marshall and Juan Verdugo were executed in San Diego for their part in the 1851 Garra Revolt.

> A reason often advanced to support the contention that Marshall advised the Indians to kill the Californians in the Pauma Massacre is that soon after he arrived at San Diego he courted Lugarda Dionisia Osuna, but that she rejected him, and he then left and went to Agua Caliente to live. The story continues that Lugarda later married José María Alvarado who was captured by the Indians at the Pauma rancho, and that Marshall ordered him killed to even the score for winning Lugarda. This hypothesis is not supportable in light of existing records, nor does it explain the deaths of the others, including Lugarda's brother, Santiago. Lugarda Dionisia Osuna was born at Mission San Juan Capistrano in 1822 and was about five years older than Marshall. She had married Alvarado on February 22, 1841, four years before Marshall arrived in San Diego, so he could not have courted her. Perhaps the story was fabricated to

62 Bibb, 1976.

63 Jasper, James A., "The Wickedest Man in California," *Los Angeles Times Magazine*, August 2, 1931.

> explain Lugarda's role in Marshall's baptism just before he was hanged in 1851. At that time, she acted as his madrina (godmother), but why she stood for him rather than someone else is unknown. It is alleged that at that time Marshall asked her to forgive him for his role in her first husband's death. Certainly, such a revelation would have been newsworthy, but no such story appears in the accounts of his execution. It can only be concluded that Marshall took no part in the Pauma Massacre.[64]

Adding credence to the rumors of insurrection, Cota moved his men northwest to Temecula after the incident, creating fear amongst the Calfornios that the Indians had aligned themselves with the Americans.[65] In response, Mexican General José María Flores at Los Angeles sent orders to Californio José del Carmen Lugo in San Bernardino, to take a contingent of men, suppress what seemed to be the beginnings of an Indian uprising, and avenge the deaths of the eleven soldiers.[66]

---

64 Ibid.

65 Lech, Steve, *Along the Old Roads: A History of the Portion of Southern California That Became Riverside County 1772-1893*. Published by the author, 2004, pp. 52-53, also see Strong 1929, p. 149.

66 Ibid.

MOUNTING TENSIONS

WHEN NEWS OF THE BATTLE OF San Pasqual and the Pauma Massacre reached the Temecula Indian village, the community responded to the region's mounting tensions by going to Pauba, a nearby secluded area, for safety.[67] Pauba, which means place of water in the 'Atáaxum language, is located east of the Temecula village and southwest of the canyon where the Temecula Massacre would take place, in an area used for pear orchards and goat herding. Aguanga, located several miles southeast of Pauba, was situated on the main road linking Los Angeles and Sonora (Gila Trail), which passed through Cupa and the Warner Springs Valley. Pauba also boasted a better tactical and defensive advantage than the Temecula Village.

Pauba had a full view of the surrounding area, being situated atop a high point with a good water supply and located adjacent to the main road, which would require travelers to pass it.[68] Later, when the surviving Temecula Indians in this area encountered the approaching Mormon Battalion, they were able to get into battle position quickly. Leader of the Battalion, Philip St. George Cooke, noted using a corral there, and described the area as a deserted ranch where the slaughter of the San Luis Indians occurred.[69]

---

67 Harrington, 1986, Volume 3, Reel 115, Frame 282.
68 Bibb, 1991.
69 Cooke, 1849, pp. 81-82.

In the months leading up to the Battle of San Pasqual and the Pauma Massacre, José del Carmen Lugo conducted numerous visits into Temecula.[70] Lugo was a wealthy Californio, and son of Don Antonio María Lugo, also known as El Viejo. The Lugos were a well-known family that owned vast tracts of land throughout Southern California. Lugo was acquainted with the area and had detailed knowledge about the Temecula Indians, knowing how large the able and equipped fighting force would have been. At that time, the population of the Temecula Indian village was around 250 to 300 people. Lugo's numerous patrols in and around Temecula during the late months of 1846 undoubtedly alerted the Luiseño and further added to the escalating tensions in the region. Lugo would later indicate that in October 1846, while in Temecula, he learned the Indians in San Bernardino "had risen and were coming to commit outrages on the ranchos," but he was able to return quickly to San Bernardino and diffuse the situation.[71] He promised the Cahuilla hundreds of head of cattle and horses in exchange for their loyalty.[72]

Figure 12: Excerpt from the genealogy chart of the Lugo Family of California for 1771-1937, showing various cattle brands within the family. University of Southern California, Digital Library.

70 Lugo, Don José del Carmon Lugo. Interview by Thomas Savage, 1877. Bancroft Library, University of California Berkeley. Translated by Beattie, 1961.

71 Ibid.

72 Harrington, 1986, Volume 3, Cahuilla, Reel 112, Frame 564.

News of the Pauma Massacre reached San Diego and Los Angeles between December 19th and 20th, 1846. General José María Flores ordered Lugo to find the Indians responsible for the Pauma Massacre and kill them. Lugo's assignment was not simply to avenge the eleven men; he was to deliver a blow to the Native community that would crush its leadership and its spirit.

When Lugo learned of the Temecula Indians' position at Pauba and that they significantly outnumbered his forces, he devised a plan to lure the Temecula men into the narrows of the canyon away from their defensible location. The canyon boasted the advantages of furrows in the bedrock that would allow them to hide his Californio and Cahuilla troops for an ambush and stage a deadly close-quarters battle. Lugo could also make up for his lack in forces by placing armed men strategically atop the canyon ridge.

The canyon itself was near the trail to Temecula but was so narrow that it was unlikely to be used as a primary route or a wagon road. A trail down the Temecula Creek would have resulted in a longer route to Temecula, been impassable and dangerous at times of inclement weather, and was inconsistent with other reports of "traveling over hills and valleys."[73] According to oral histories from the Tribe, as unease spread through the region, a group of Temecula warriors were preparing their weapons and a quiver sprang to life, as if invigorated from the sinew it was made from, and pointed toward the direction of the canyon. Some interpreted this as a sign that the battle outcome would be favorable, but tribal elders cautioned that this was a portent of disaster.[74]

The Temecula force was comprised of warriors and the leadership from neighboring villages. For safety, most people in the Temecula Village left for Pauba Village nearby. In the 1950s, local historian Horace Parker interviewed Pechanga member Antonio "Tony"

73 Miller, Anne J., *The Southern Emigrant Trail through Riverside County*. Author House: Bloomington, IN. 2012, p. 31.

74 Macarro, Mark, Pechanga Tribal Chairman, Interview April 19, 2019.

Figure 13: Tony Ashman. Pechanga Tribal historian and leader, circa 1930. Pechanga Cultural Resources Department, Raymond Basquez, Sr. Collection.

Ashman, who was born in 1879, about the massacre. Ashman told Parker the following first-hand account he heard from Tribal elder, Leon Yuhac, whose actions could have possibly prevented the massacre:

> When [Leon] was a young man he worked on the Santa Margarita Rancho. One day he was given an excellent horse and a message which he was to deliver to some Californians encamped near Temecula. He was also given explicit directions as to which trail to follow to find the Californians and he was not to deviate from it. He followed orders and found the Californios.

Figure 14: Leon Yuhac was sent from Rancho Santa Margarita with a message that might have prevented the massacre, but he never delivered the letter. Pechanga Cultural Resources Department, Stubblefield Collection.

After resting overnight, he was given a return message and once again admonished not to make any side trips. The young man was a Temecula and, with a top horse, he could make good time; so in spite of the warnings to the contrary, he decided to make a side trip and visit his home at the Temecula Indian village. When he arrived, he found the village deserted. Searching through the Rancheria, he heard some low moanings in one of the adobes. Entering it, he found an old, infirm Indian woman almost dead from thirst and hunger. He asked her where the people had gone but she was too weak to speak. The young man brought her some water from the creek and mixed her a gruel or seed flour that he found in the house. Regaining strength, but still too weak to talk, she pointed toward the Negro Canyon which forms

> the northeastern portal into the Temecula Valley. With this news, frightened by the still unexplained deserted village, and with no time to investigate, he continued on to Santa Margarita.[75]

This story corroborates Lugo's account that Californio leader José Ramon Carrillo and his forces were at San Luis Rey. Lugo was known to be a cautious man. He understood that his small force would be bested if faced in an open battlefield. When he discovered that he and his men were significantly outnumbered, Lugo sent a message to Carrillo asking for reinforcements. In Lugo's description of the massacre, he notes that the Temecula fighters positioned themselves at the front of the line and the tribal elders and leadership were in the middle with the ultimate objective being to lure the fighters out of their prime location.

A tense social undercurrent pervaded California during the Mexican-American War. Mexicans had recently gained possession of the territory from Spain twenty-five years prior and in the following period Californian society became profit-driven with the booming cattle economy and land grab. The use of Indian labor was ubiquitous; however, there was an underlying fear amongst Mexican-Californio rancho owners that a unified Indian uprising could effectively eliminate the Mexican presence in Alta California. In 1846, Indians outnumbered Californios, and the region was far removed from the Mexican capital and the government's sphere of influence. During the war, it was paramount for Mexican-Californios to demonstrate power and control over these tribes.

75 Parker, 1963, p. 17.

THE TEMECULA MASSACRE

Thomas Savage chronicled Lugo's firsthand account of the Temecula Massacre in 1877. The interview was collected for use as source material in Hubert Howe Bancroft's *History of California* series and was later translated from Spanish to English by Helen Pruitt Beattie in the late 1950s. Titled *Vida de un Ranchero,* or *Life of a Rancher,* Lugo discusses several events in his life, including a detailed account of the Battle of Chino. This skirmish between Californios and American sympathizers in September 1846 is significant in that it was during this encounter Lugo was able to commandeer "a great many firearms and ammunition."[76] It was with this supply of arms that gave his forces the upper hand against the Temecula Indians.

When Lugo arrived at Santa Gertrudis, an established camp located near present-day Murrieta Hot Springs, also referred to as Adobe Springs and called Tótpa by the 'Atáaxum, he had accumulated a force of about twenty men. It was on a reconnaissance mission that Lugo discovered he and his men were outnumbered, and he knew if they were to pursue the Temecula warriors in an open battlefield, his

76 Beattie, 1961.

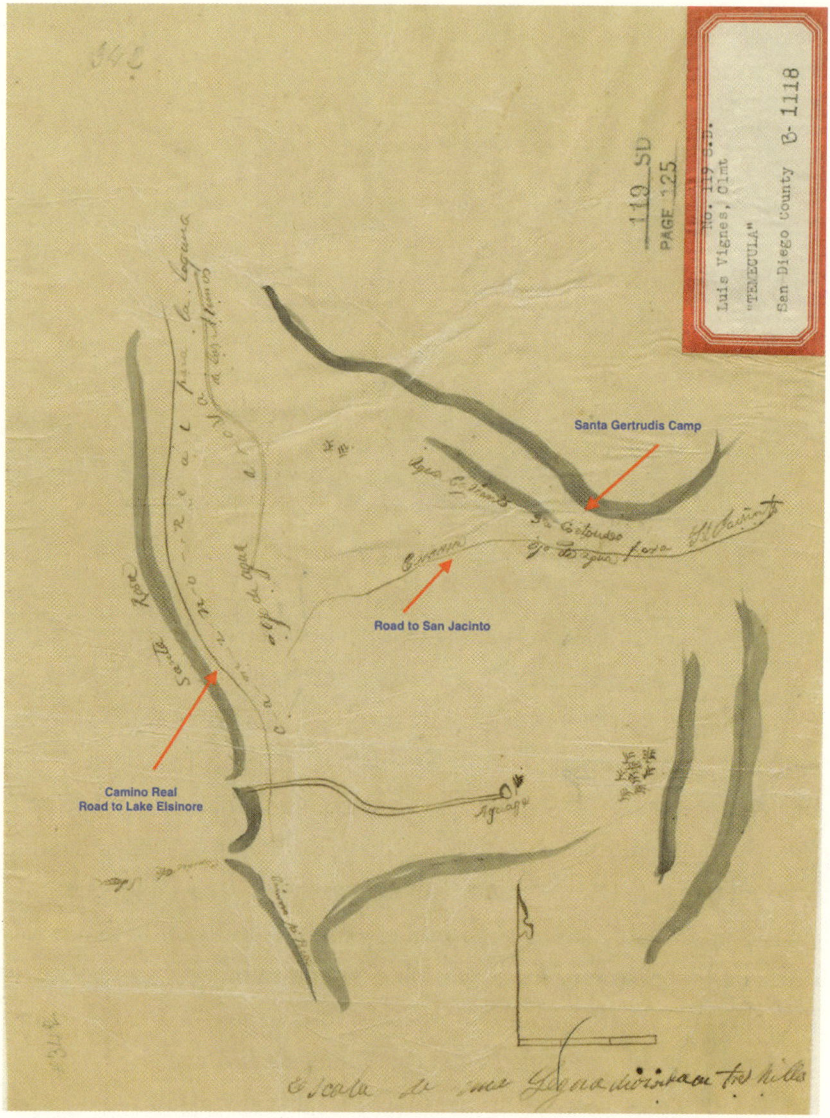

Figure 15a. Excerpt of the Diseño del Rancho Temecula with the Gertrudis Ojo de Agua or the St. Gertrudis springs are identified, c. 1840. California State Archives, Diseños Collection, #119.

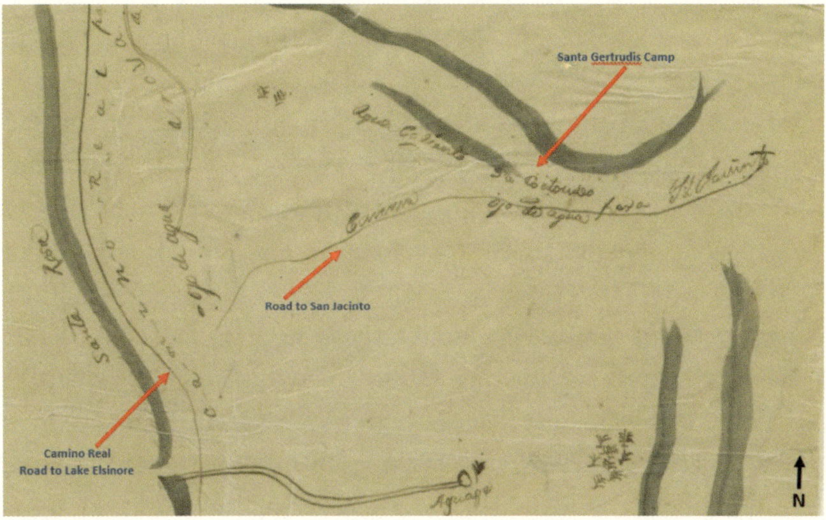

Figure 15b.

men would be in a weak defensive position. Lugo in turn sent word to Ramon Carrillo in San Luis Rey, asking for reinforcements. When only ten additional men arrived from San Luis Rey, Lugo, still leery about his chances, sought additional support from the Cahuilla tribe. Even though the Native people were viewed as childlike and unintelligent, the Californios knew they possessed a "fierce character," which was demonstrated in "many instances" after their release from Mission servitude in 1834.[77] This was also remarked upon later, when the Mormon Battalion arrived in the Temecula Valley and mistook the Native villagers as Californios, because they moved into an organized military formation, not expected from Indian people.

Lugo went north to Politana, near the present town of Colton, to call upon Cahuilla Indian Chief Juan Antonio for assistance. Juan Antonio was loyal to the Lugo family and was guardian of the family's large land holdings. By the early 1840s, raids on California ranchos by Indians from the Colorado River area, and as far away as Utah, had

77 Hayes, 1976, p.286.

become a serious issue amongst the Californio landholders.[78] In an effort to protect their lands, the Lugo family enlisted the services of Juan Antonio who led a group of Cahuilla Indians from the San Jacinto Mountains.[79] During the Mexican-American War, Juan Antonio remained loyal to the Lugos, and after the war, he went back to policing Lugo's lands and livestock. Juan Antonio and a force of about fifty men set off for Temecula to join Carrillo and Lugo's men at the Santa Gertrudis camp to prepare for the attack. The force fighting on behalf of the Mexican side then totaled approximately eighty men.

Later, in 1933, John P. Harrington's Luiseño consultant Juan Sotelo Calac would share information passed to him through the oral tradition about the Massacre and the Cahuilla involvement. Calac relayed to Harrington that the ruse to get Temecula Indians into the canyon began with a group of Juan Antonio's men calling out to them in the Luiseño language. They said, "Come over here, friends! We have a matter to discuss. Namely about how we are going to massacre the

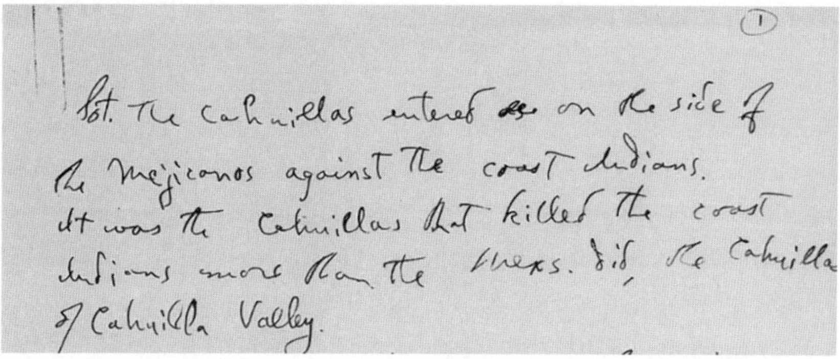
1
Sot. The Cahuillas entered on the side of the Mejicanos against the coast Indians. It was the Cahuillas that killed the coast Indians more than the Mexs. did, the Cahuilla of Cahuilla Valley.

Figure 16: "Sot [Juan Sotelo Calac] the Cahuillas entered on the side of the Mejicanos against the coast Indians [Luiseño]. It was the Cahuillas that killed the coast Indians more than the Mexs. did, the Cahuilla of Cahuilla Valley." John Peabody Harrington's Field Notes, Luiseño. National Anthropological Archives, Smithsonian Institution. Volume 3, Reel 115, Frame 282.

78 James, Harry C., *The Cahuilla Indians*, Westlake Press. 1960, p. 113.
79 Ibid.

Mexicans."[80] The Temecula Indians under the leadership of Manuelito Cota would follow them, the men said, because the Indians of the Cahuilla Valley were their paisanos [countrymen].[81] Lugo and Carrillo stationed themselves in the canyon and feigned retreat in order to lead the Luiseño force into the ambush. Survivors of the Massacre told Tony Ashman the men were lured out of safety by a group of Californios feigning fatigue. Thinking they had the upper hand, a large number of the Luiseño men charged, against Manuelito's commands, only to be attacked by the Cahuilla lying in wait. The Californios then mounted and turned back to fight the Temeculas from the front while the men hiding among the rocks and brush closed in from behind.[82]

There is further speculation as to why the Cahuilla agreed to fight against the Temecula Indians, with whom they had long-standing familial connections. According to Ashman, the motivation for the betrayal may have stemmed from a previous, deadly ambush orchestrated by Temecula Indians against the Cahuilla, which occurred prior to Spanish contact. The two tribes may have seen each other as traditional enemies; additionally, Ashman also speculated the Cahuilla may have been bribed by Lugo. The Cahuilla, like the Temecula Indians, may have viewed this as an opportunity to make a political stand, and to demonstrate their allegiance to the Mexican cause.

In 1920, John Harrington interviewed an elder from San Juan Capistrano, José de la Cruz, who was familiar with the event, described Juan Antonio's role in the Temecula Massacre:

> Juan Antonio lived over the mountains beyond Temecula. He was a leader and had a hundred men all armed with bows and arrows. Their arrows they carried

80 The statement in Luiseño reads, "*tceyk, no-peywum, tcumtcumteéla míika, tcamtéela, tcunxe'éepe cucáavitmi.*" Linguistic translation provided by Eric Elliot, Linguist for Pechanga Tribal Government, May 2021.

81 Harrington, 1986, Volume 3, Reel 115, Frame 282; Strong 1929, p. 149.

82 Hudson 1989, p. 29.

in the hide of a deer, and entire hide made into a sack that held a hundred arrows and hung on the back to the left so that by reaching over the left shoulder with the right hand the arrows could be drawn out and fitted to the bow quickly. His men were well clothed in *gamuza* [buckskin] and were strong fighters.

The Pala Indians and those about Temecula were angry with the Mexicans that lived here on the coast and when these went over to Pala the Indians there took them and tortured and killed them.[83] The Mexicans wanted to fight the Indians of Pala [Luiseño] and went over the mountains to Juan Antonio and promised him 500 head of cattle and 200 head of horses if he would take his men to Temecula and kill Indians there. He agreed to do it. Then the Indians of Pala not knowing that the Mexicans had treated [sic] with Juan Antonio sent men to ask him to fight the Mexicans. He did not say much, but the Indians thought he was on their side. Then the Mexicans went over to Pala and the Indians there began to chase them and they went northeast. Juan Antonio had come and hid in a *barranoco* [ravine] and the Indians of Pala thought he would fight the Mexicans. When they came up to him, he let the Mexicans pass him by, and when the Indians drew near to where he was hiding he suddenly rushed out with all his men and killed very many of them.[84]

83 This is in reference to the Pauma Massacre.

84 This interview with José de la Gracia Cruz (Acú) describes the Temecula Indians as the Indians of Pala, meaning "Luiseños." *John Peabody Harrington Papers*, 1907-1959, documents on file at Pechanga Cultural Resources Department. The Papers of John Peabody Harrington in the Smithsonian Institution, 1907-1957, Volume 3.

On December 31, 1846, while the American Army and Navy forces were moving north from San Diego to Los Angeles, they camped near present day Rancho Bernardo. Dr. John S. Griffin noted "the Mexicans and a party of Indians had attacked the Indians about Warner's Ranch and killed some thirty of them. These Indians are our friends, and have most certainly been encouraged to take up arms in our favour [sic] and I should think ought to be supported…it is said that there are now in our neighborhood some 70 Californians and 300 Indians in arms."[85] Based on the date of Griffin's report, it is likely that the Temecula Massacre occurred in late December 1846.

Lugo's first-hand account of the Temecula Massacre is as follows:

> The messenger would have to take three days or more to go and return, losing more than a day uselessly. Before he came back, I heard that Ramon Carrillo was in San Luis Rey with ten men. I sent word for him to come, and he came immediately with his men. I ordered him to watch the Indians, and I left that same hour for Jurupa where I could enlist an Indian Chief named Juan Antonio. We went together to Temecula, carrying two pieces of white cloth to use as a special signal to Juan Antonio's Indians. We reached Santa Gertrudis and rejoined Ramon Carrillo and his force. We notified our people that we were leaving immediately, to fight the hostile Indians at daybreak. We started at eleven o'clock at night.
>
> It was daylight when we came to the enemy. We arranged our plan of attack. There were high hills and deep canons, but not extensive. In one of the canyons from which we could reach the enemy, I placed an

85 Griffin, John S., *A Doctor Comes to California*, San Francisco: California Historical Society, 1953, p. 345.

ambuscade of fifty Indians and fifteen white men, with strict orders to not show themselves until the last of the Indian enemies passed.

I stationed myself in the canyon with some men, and Carrillo went to trick the enemy by calling their attention and leading them to follow him. As soon as they saw him, they rose and went after him. He passed them, fired at them, and retreated slowly and in an orderly manner until he came to where I was. The Indians followed him eagerly. My men who had rifles and other good arms, of whom I had placed five on ridges or high places in the canon [sic], were told to fire only at the fighters because they were the chiefs and came only in the middle of the main body.

We lured them on about a league until they passed the ambuscade. Then the men rushed out from the ambush upon them from the back at the same time that we fought them from the front.

We made a great slaughter, and falling upon them from the rear killed many of them. Before reaching Aguanga in their flight, eighteen or twenty of them turned back and gave up their arms. They were made prisoners and placed in charge of Chief Juan Antonio, who told me to care for my men and he would care for the prisoners.

On reaching Aguanga we amused ourselves killing some three Indians who continued fighting. After terminating the affair, in which perhaps a hundred Indians perished, we went back to Juan Antonio and found he had killed all the prisoners. I reproached him for these acts of cruelty, and he answered me very coolly, that he had gone to hunt and fight and kill Indians who would

> kill him; that he was sure that if they had caught him they would not have spared his life but would have burned him alive.[86]

Lugo censured Juan Antonio for killing the captives, but ultimately rewarded him. Juan Antonio's rationale was that Lugo was a captain of the white men, and he himself was a captain of the Indians; an important distinction.[87] According to Griffin's report, Juan Antonio perceived the killing of the Luiseño prisoners as worthy cause, in that if the circumstances were reversed, they would have done the same.

Figure 17: View west from Vail Lake, circa 1950. (A) Temecula Village approximate location. (B) Pauba approximate location at base of foothills. (C) Santa Gertrudis camp approximate location. (D) Canyon where the ambush occurred. From the collections of the Temecula Valley Museum.

86 Beattie, 1950, pp. 207-210.
87 James, 1960, p. 115.

Six of Lugo's men were wounded, but no deaths were recorded of his men. Juan Antonio's horse, mounted with his prized silver saddle, was killed from under him, but he was able to commandeer another mount and leave the canyon with his prisoners.

Later, Diego Sepulveda arrived with twenty-five additional men from Los Angeles. Believing that retaliation was eminent, they returned to the canyon only to discover that only the old and infirm remained.[88]

American judge Benjamin Hayes noted of the Temecula Massacre that:

> "...it might commemorate the bloody battle that took place near Ahuanga [sic], in January 1847, between the Cahuillas under their famed chief, Juan Antonio, and the insurrectionary San Luiseños, commanded by Manuelito Cota and young Pablo Apis. This was a sequel to the massacre of Pauma, in the month of December previous. The Cahuillas really were led by a Californian, Don José del Carmen Lugo, of Los Angeles, and placed themselves in an ambuscade. Don Ramon Carrillo, at the head of a strong party of native Californians, attacked the Indians of Apis. These retreating without thought fell into the hands of the Cahuillas who showed no mercy; *great numbers were slain.*"[89]

Contemporary documentation of the massacre during that time recognized the event as a proxy battle of the Mexican-American War. California and U.S. history books and accounts of this war rarely make mention of it, and yet Native accounts and those from participants not only demonstrate specific details of the event, but also carry

88 Beattie, 1950, p. 210.

89 Hayes, Benjamin, *Pioneer Notes from the Diaries of Judge Benjamin Hayes, 1849-1875*, Arno Press, New York, reprint 1976. (Emphasis added.)

evidence that although the battle was anticipated, an ambush betrayal was not.

Most accounts state that the warriors entered the canyon on foot and horseback pursuing the Californians for a few miles until they reached an open valley (present-day Vail Lake). Others indicate that the Temecula Massacre site might have been located further southeast; but this estimation does not account for the Temecula force originating at Pauba. Other accounts suggest the battlefield corridor spans many miles, primarily along the historic route to the village of Aguanga, and there are possibly several locations where altercations occurred.

Figure 18: View of Temecula Creek flooding in 1926. Temecula Valley Museum, Wilkinson Collection.

Historic maps and other sources identify the area where the massacre took place as Cañón del Negro, Negro Canyon or "N— Canyon." The name of the canyon was derived from a prosperous African American family who attempted to settle in the area during the nineteenth century, but were forced to relocate upon discovering their lands were a part of the Pauba Rancho. The narrow terminus of this corridor was later dammed off and filled to create Vail Lake in 1947. Historic photographs and aerial imagery of the canyon, taken just prior to the dam's construction, show the winding canyon approximately six miles in length with narrow dugouts and hollows throughout. Historic photographs from the 1920s demonstrate the canyon's erosion from seasonal flooding.

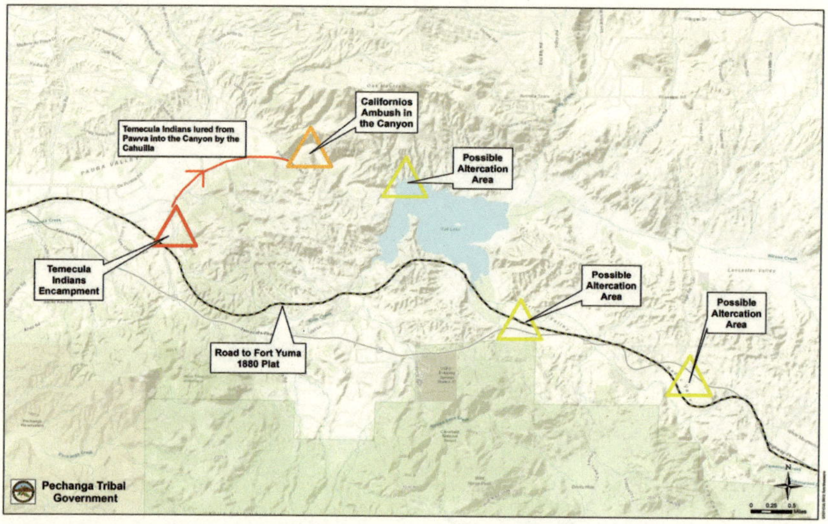

Figure 19: Approximate locations of battle movements during the massacre. Prepared by Shelly Knight, Pechanga GIS Department.

As a result of this, the current canyon floor, as seen in aerial photographs from the 1920s, is several feet lower than its position would have been in 1846. An archaeological survey conducted in 1947 indicated that "the sands of the mesa at the junction of Arroyo Seco and the Temecula River show the results of shifting by powerful flood waters."[90] Even following the construction of the Vail Lake dam, the region experienced several additional catastrophic floods in 1969 and 1993. The 1969 flood was so immense that the Vail Lake dam failed, and portions of the spillway had to be rebuilt.

Remaining archaeological evidence of the battle has likely been widely dispersed throughout the area and within the strata of the canyon itself. The 1947 survey identified seventeen archaeological sites within the basin. According to Tony Ashman, sun-bleached bones could be seen littered throughout the canyon for years, and Vail Ranch employee Louis Roripaugh noted that bones were still visible in the valley near the cemetery in the 1960s and 1970s. During construction of the dam, Roripaugh managed the work crew excavating the canyon walls. From his own estimate, the river bench was hundreds of feet above the present canyon floor, and that during the excavation process they went through only a few inches of top soil followed by several feet deep of river gravel.[91]

Despite questions about the specific sites of the massacre, it seems certain that the ambush occurred as follows: The Cahuilla ended their mock retreat and proceeded to fight, and at the same time a group of hidden men emerged from the rear of the Luiseño force and began to fire upon them. When the Indians turned to escape, they found all their exits blocked by the deadly fire of the Californios.[92] Men positioned along the canyon ridge fired

90 McCown, Benjamin Ernest, Collected Papers of Benjamin Ernest McCown, Paper Number Six. "Archaeological Survey of Pauba Flood Control Basin." Archaeological Survey Association of Southern California. 1964.

91 *Parker, Horace*, "The Brush Country Journal." October 14, 1956, p. 38.

92 Parker, 1963, p. 18.

down upon them. When the Temecula warriors were trapped, Juan Antonio and his men charged. Mistaking Antonio and the Cahuillas for allies, the Temecula warriors rallied briefly; no doubt calling to acquaintances among the Cahuillas and envisioning a glorious victory.[93] Shockingly, instead the Cahuilla began killing the Temecula Indians, a turn of events that resulted in multiple exists from the battlefield with each man fleeing for his life.[94]

The Cahuillas, led by Juan Antonio, sought to kill those in hiding. The slaughter raged for hours, driving the remnants of the Temecula warriors and their allies up through the canyon, into the valley, and toward Aguanga. Pauma Rancho grantee José Antonio Serrano was known to have expressed regret about the escape of the young Pablo Apis from the Temecula Massacre; and notes that while the rangers killed Apis' horse, Apis himself managed to escape.[95]

According to Tony Ashman, the grandfather of Pechanga Tribal Member Celestino Pajanem concealed himself along the route of the massacre and observed his brother pursued by mounted Californians.[96]

> "The brother was on foot and was soon overtaken by the mounted men and, as he watched, the Californians drove their lances into the cringing body of the defeated man. The Viejo told Mr. Ashman he still had his bow and arrows in his fist, [and his] impulse was to run to the assistance of his doomed brother. As he grasped his bow there flashed before his eyes a mental picture of his children and the question of what would become of them if he were killed. So closing his eyes to shut out

93 Ibid.

94 Ibid.

95 Morrison, Lorrin L., *Warner: The Man and the Ranch*, Los Angeles, California, 1962, p. 38.

96 Hicks 1970, p. 46.

> the scene before him, he sank back into his place of concealment and survived the massacre."[97]

Many of the slain remained where they lay up until the arrival of the Mormon Battalion on January 25, 1847. The Temecula Indians who survived the ambush went to Warner's Ranch and hid in the canyons and hills until the Mormon Battalion, traveling through the area, came upon them.

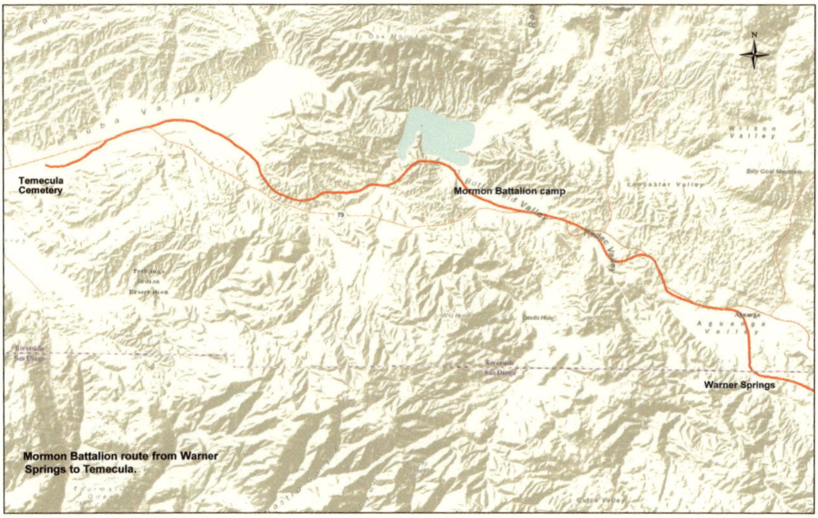

Figure 20. Estimated route of the Mormon Battalion from Warner's Ranch and the Indian Village near Agua Caliente along the Yuma Trail to Los Angeles. Map composite generated from 1857, 1878, 1880, 1884, and 1896 Plat Maps. Created by Shelly Knight, Pechanga GIS Department 2020.

97 Parker, 1963, p. 20.

HISTORICAL RECKONING

After the massacre, relations between the Temecula and Cahuilla became further strained, already having reasons to be tense. According to one of Harrington's Cahuilla consultants, a prior massacre had occurred in San Timoteo Canyon under the direction of Cabezon, a contemporary of Juan Antonio's who was the leader of another Cahuilla Band. Talking to Harrington in the 1930s, the consultant stated: "that's why we have the San Luiseños as enemies all the time."[98] Because of these incidents and undoubtedly others never undocumented, a dark motto evolved among the Temecula Indians to *never trust a Cahuilla.*[99] The Temecula Indians and their allies were beaten and betrayed by the Cahuillas. This sentiment dissipated when the late nineteenth and twentieth centuries brought new challenges for both tribes. Relations between the two tribes are amicable today.

Since the 1870s, historians focused primarily on the Battle of San Pasqual, including cursory information about the Temecula Massacre. Accounts of the events are found piecemeal in various documents, diaries, and oral recordings. One secondary source begins

98 This interview with Lee Arenas of Palm Springs describes Cabezon's roll in the San Timoteo Canyon massacre and Juan Antonio's attack on the Luiseño. *John Peabody Harrington Papers*, 1907-1959, documents on file at Pechanga Cultural Resources Department. The Papers of John Peabody Harrington in the Smithsonian Institution, 1907-1957, Volume 3, Reel 114, Frame 421.

99 Strong 1929, p. 149.

with a brief mention in Hubert Howe Bancroft's *History of California* series stemming from Lugo's interview with Thomas Savage in 1877 and later in Millard F. Hudson's 1907 article on the Pauma Massacre for *The Southern California Quarterly* journal. During the 1930s, historian Winifred Dodson wrote several articles on the subject for the *San Diego Union Tribune* series "Old Tales of the Southwest."

Of all the historians to analyze the Temecula Massacre, Horace Parker has been the most prolific. A veterinarian by trade, he dedicated much of his life to investigating Southern California and Temecula history. Many of his descriptions were written for the "Brush Country Journal" a local history series published in the *Riverside Daily Press* newspaper (which later became the *Press Enterprise*) during the 1950s and 1960s. These articles capitalized on the popularity of western history and were a mixture of Parker's histories and stories from his travels throughout Southern California. Parker's 1971 book, *The Historic Valley of Temecula: The Temecula Massacre,* gathered all of these articles together. In the numerous iterations of the event, Parker's narrative is largely consistent, heavily relying on Lugo's first-hand account and the interviews he conducted with Pechanga elder, Antonio Ashman, who heard these accounts from his elders. Parker described the Luiseño's tactics as "poor at best" and that, "helter-skelter, the Indians tossed discipline to the winds."[100]

However, Parker's view conflicts with other accounts from 1847, which show the Luiseño as a highly organized group who were able to form battle formations quickly and described as well versed in "Mexican military tactics."[101] Further, Parker maintained that the Temecula Indians had initially entrenched themselves in the canyon, which is where they planned to stage their attack against the Californios; not at the more defensible location at Pauba. Parker also

100 *Riverside Daily Press (Press Enterprise)*, "The Brush Country Journal." November 9, 1956, Part 15.

101 Brown, James S. Life of a Pioneer: *The Autobiography of James S. Brown*. Salt Lake City, Cannon & Sons Co., 1900, p. 72.

claims that the Indians were lured from the shelter of the canyon into a region called "Long Valley," where the massacre, according to some accounts, occurred. However, this location identifier does not align with Lugo's statements, placing himself within the canyon with men stationed along the canyon ridge, using the members of the neighboring Cahuilla Tribe to lure the Temecula Indians *into* the canyon. Since Parker obtained much of his information from Tony Ashman, who in turn heard these narratives passed through the oral tradition from Tribal elders, most of whom were too young to have participated, makes these accounts 3rd or 4th hand, which may have altered some details of the event.

THE MORMON BATTALION

The Mormon Battalion were the first recorded travelers through the area after the Temecula Massacre, arriving at Warner's Ranch on January 21, 1847. Only a few months prior, in July 1846, the Mormon Battalion was formed and recruited by Colonel Philip St. George Cooke at Council Bluffs, Iowa, as a unit of the Army of the West. Their mission was to follow Kearny's troops to establish a wagon road and provide additional forces in Alta California. This road later became the Southern Emigrant Trail through Yuma, the Colorado River, with a stop at Warner's Ranch and several others in Southern California. A few women and pioneers accompanied the group on their journey from Council Bluffs to San Diego. Most notably, Captain Jesse D. Hunter's wife Lydia Hunter gave birth to the "first American born in San Diego" shortly after the Battalion's arrival, but she died in childbirth and is buried in Point Loma, San Diego.

According to Sergeant, Daniel Tyler, when the Battalion arrived at Warner's Ranch there were a number of Temecula Indians there. Tyler remarks:

> They were friendly to the United States government, and had recently captured, brought here, and killed some ten or eleven Californians. They had, however lost

> thirty-eight of their own number, killed by Californians and some other hostile tribe in retaliation, in Temecula Valley, who lay in ambush and took them by surprise. These Indians begged the Colonel to allow them to accompany the Battalion, that they might bury their dead on the way, and the Colonel consented.[102]

Mormon Battalion member Robert Bliss describes the troops' encounter at Warner's Ranch as they were "encamped in a beautiful valley where we met encamped 200 or 300 Indians who have assisted us in the War."[103] His description is significant, in that the Temecula Indians were perceived as allies to the United States and engaged in battles to defeat the Mexican forces. More importantly, it demonstrates a level of Indian agency that is diminished in many historical accounts.

In Colonel Cooke's diary, he mentions that while his men were assembling at Warner's Ranch, over a hundred Indians, some from the area and others from "lower down," wished to go with him to the valley to bury their dead. In addition, while at Warner's Ranch, Cooke met with Chief Juan Bautista of the Los Coyotes Cahuilla, a group separate from the Cahuilla who had fought under Juan Antonio's leadership. In his dialogue with Bautista about the Temecula Massacre, Cooke told Bautista that he "regretted that any part of his nation should have taken so unwise a course in favor of the Californians, who would now abandon them."[104] With the close of the war eminent, Cooke encouraged them to return home.

Based on various journal accounts, Cooke sent an advance guard ahead of the larger Mormon Battalion party to assist with the burying

102 Tyler, Sergeant Daniel, *A Concise History of the Mormon Battalion in the Mexican War 1846-1847.* Salt Lake City. The reference to the Californians killed at Warner's Ranch became known as the Pauma Massacre. 1881, p. 250.

103 Robert Bliss Journal, MS 79, San Diego History Center Document Collection, San Diego, CA.

104 Cooke, 1849, p. 82.

of the Temecula Massacre victims. This group appears to have included Mormon Battalion members Henry Standage, Levi Hancock, Jean Baptiste Charbonneau, and a group of unnamed Native men. Levi Hancock, stated on January 22, 1847, "Mr. Shauino [Charbonneau] tells me that tomorrow we go down and help bury some dead Indians, who have been killed in battle about 30 [in number], two weeks ago."[105]

Jean Baptiste Charbonneau, Sacajawea's and Toussaint Charbonneau's son, served as a guide to Cooke during the years 1846-47.[106] The Mormon Battalion was set to follow the route taken by Kearny's Army of the West; however, Charbonneau advised Cooke to pursue a different route, and Cooke heavily relied on Charbonneau's guidance.[107] The guide skillfully selected the route of the battalion, hunted for their provisions, found camps, scouted, and fought with Native groups, making it easier for Cooke to bring his half-starved group of 350 on the 1,200-mile journey through hostile territory to San Diego.[108]

The advance guard departed Warner's Ranch on January 23rd. According to Standage's diary entry on that same date, he states, "Left Warners [sic] early. I was detailed for a guard; marched in the advance all day."[109] Accounts indicate that on January 23rd, the bulk of the Battalion led by Cooke with Antonio Garra, Chief of the Agua Calientes, traveled about eighteen miles, and the advance guard traveled about

105 Hancock, Levi, Levi W. Hancock Journal 1846-1847, MSS SC 3252, L. Tom Perry Special Collections, Harold B. Lee Library, Brigham Young University, Provo, Utah. Hancock's journal is also transcribed in the *The Saving Sacrifice of the Mormon Battalion from the Journals of Levi Ward Hancock*, ed. Herbert A Hancock, Utah: Bystander at Large Productions, 2000. This document's transcription more accurately reflects Hancock's January 22, 1847 journal entry. (Emphasis added.)

106 Charbonneau was named "alcalde" of Mission San Luis Rey in November 1847, but only remained in the position for one year.

107 Reading, James, "Jean Baptiste Charbonneau," *Journal of San Diego History*, San Diego Historical Society Quarterly, March 1965, Volume 11, Number 2.

108 Ibid.

109 Standage, Henry, Diary of Henry Standage, Company "E," Mormon Battalion. Manuscripts on file, San Diego Historical Society Research Archives.

twenty-five miles.[110] Both the advance guard and the main body of the battalion would have passed Indian villages in Oak Grove, Aguanga, and $óova, which is located at the crossing point of the Temecula creek.

A storm began on the afternoon of the 23rd and lasted into the next day, hindering the groups' progress to only three and four miles on the 24th.[111] Nathaniel V. Jones of the Mormon Battalion described the night of the 23rd as follows:

> We camped in a small valley close in by the side of a small mountain. It commenced raining just that night and continued to rain all night. There was an Indian came to us that night who appeared very friendly and he would not leave us that night, but laid all night on the ground before out tent, and it rained and the wind blew a gale until morning, then we gave him some meat for which he appeared very thankful. The Indians, a few days before we came to Warner's had taken eleven Spaniards and killed them in cold blood, the Spaniards had killed some forty of the Indians for it. They probably thought that we were their friends and would kill off the Spaniards.[112]

During times of rain, the Yuma Trail to Los Angeles or the Southern Emigrant Trail would become impassible in the present-day Vail Lake area, and an alternate route would be used through Dry Wash to Dripping Springs past the Blue Cut to the Pear Tree Spring and then

110 According to Henry Standage the advance guard traveled twenty-five miles, nd Cooke's party traveled about eighteen miles. The description identifies a man named Juan Antonio as accompanying the group. Research indicates this is not Juan Antonio of the Cahuilla tribe; rather, Antonio Garra of the Agua Caliente tribe.

111 Tyler, 1881, p. 251; Standage.

112 Jones, Nathaniel V., Nathaniel V. Jones Journal with the Mormon Battalion. 1847. *Utah Historical Quarterly* Vol. I-VI, p. 11.

onto Temecula.[113] The severity of the winter of 1846-1847 was felt throughout the state, and while the Mormon Battalion was slogging through the Southern Emigrant Trail, the Donner Party was trapped in snow in the Sierra Nevada mountain range. Frémont even noted that this winter was one of the most severe ever seen on the West Coast, and that even traveling in the low country in large groups was made difficult by "prolonged easterly storms, during which cold rains flooded the country."[114]

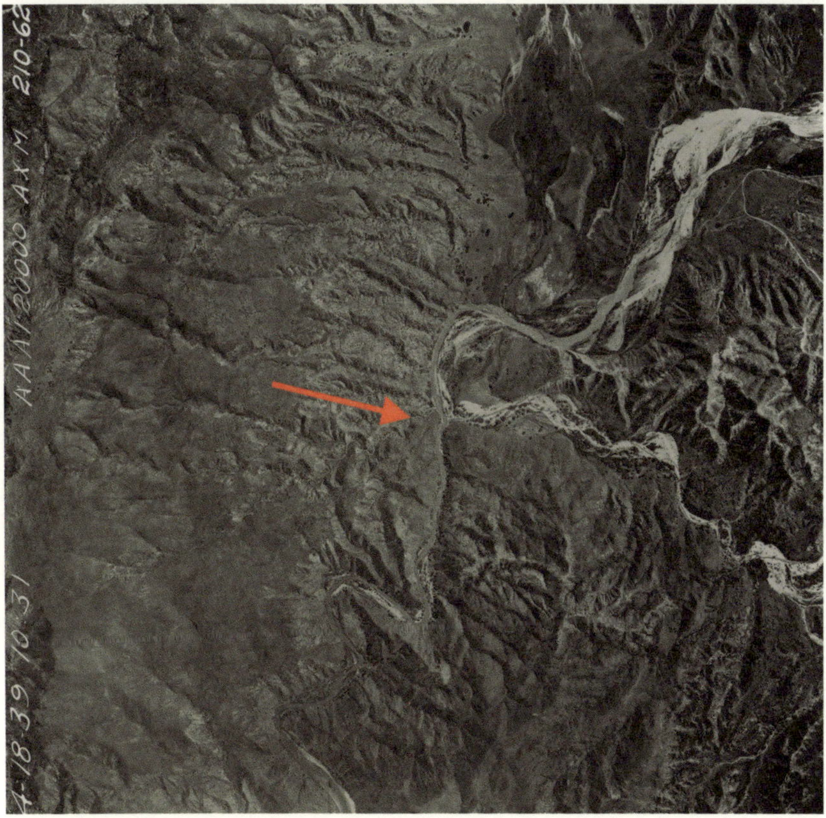

Figure 21: Aerial photograph of the Canyon prior to construction of Vail Lake, 1939. c-5750_210-62, 1939. Courtesy of University of California, Santa Barbara Library Geospatial Collection.

113 Parker, 1956.
114 Frémont, 1887, p. 592.

Figure 22: Vail Lake Dam construction, 1940s. Courtesy of Temecula Valley Museum, Wilkinson/Hancock Collection.

Cooke's January 24th entry details the impact of the storm on the Battalion's progress: "The road was very heavy...the advance guard and pioneers went nearly a mile further, and worked at a spot which they reported would have been impassable in the state of the road, as was, also this mountain torrent, now roaring behind my camp."[115]

On January 25th, the Battalion traveled on to Temecula, passing the area near what is now Vail Lake. In reference to the canyon and Temecula Creek, Levi Hancock observed that it would have been easy to build a dam between the hills that could supply water for the valley below them.[116] A dam was actually built in this location 100 years later. That night, Hancock also sketched a map of the mountains as seen from their camp.

115 Cooke, 1849, p. 81.

116 Hancock, Levi Ward, *The Saving Sacrifice of the Mormon Battalion from the Journals of Levi Ward Hancock*, ed. Herbert A Hancock, Utah: Bystander at Large Productions, 2000, p. 226.

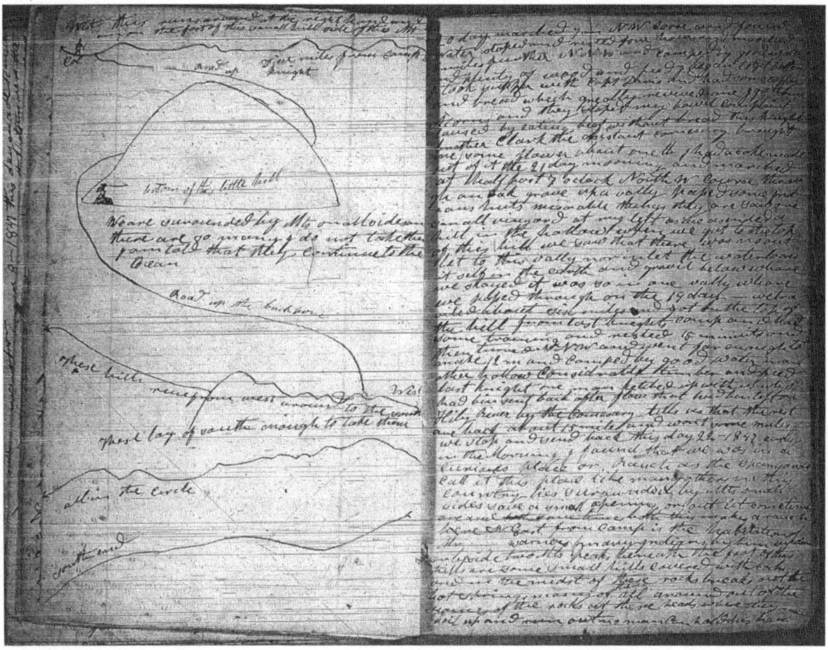

Figure 23: Levi Hancock sketched a map of the mountains as seen from the camp on the night of January 25 in the Temecula Valley, 1847. L. Tom Perry Special Collections, Harold B. Lee Library, MSS SC 3252, Brigham Young University.[117]

When the Battalion reencountered the party that came to bury the dead, a group of approximately 150, a brief moment of confusion ensued. Cooke stated that "*the party come to bury the bones* arrived this evening a little before me," and that he saw them "marching in regular file, and form a line across the road.[118] We could see the glitter of arms, and the galloping of men about the array; a drum was also

117 The notes on the Hancock sketch read "West this runs around at the right than land – and on the foot of this is a small hill side of this Mt. – Rout up – Five miles from Camp knight – bottom of this little hill – We are surrounded by Mts on all sides and there are so many I do not take them – I am told that they continue to the – Ocean –Road up the buck bone – These hills run from west around to the south –these lay of south enough to take them – all in the circle – south end."

118 Cooke, 1849, p. 82. (Emphasis added.)

Figure 24: Treaty of Cahuenga: "The Capitulation of the Mexican Army at Cahuenga" by Carl Oscar Borg. Courtesy of University of Southern California Libraries and California Historical Society. Digitally reproduced by the USC Digital Library, Image CHS-9522.

beating; few believed we were about to have an action."[119] When the Battalion was recognized, the battle formation ceased.

Upon reaching Temecula Village, the Battalion found the Temecula people were gathered to bury the dead.[120] James S. Brown of the Mormon Battalion recalled in his autobiography that on this night the two groups camped not far from one another, and friendly visits were made back and forth all evening.[121] Brown also described the Temecula Indians as dressed and armed the same as the Mexicans, and that "they displayed bravery, and some skill in Mexican military tactics."[122] The Mormon Battalion pressed on and arrived at the San Luis Rey Mission on the January 27, 1847.

It is important to note that just two weeks prior to the Battalion's arrival, on January 13, 1847, the Capitulation of Cahuenga, the agreement to cease fire, was signed by John C. Frémont and Andres Pico. A year later, on February 2, 1848, the two countries would sign the Treaty of Guadalupe Hidalgo, which formally ended the war and ceded Mexico's northern provinces to the United States.

119 Ibid.
120 Tyler, 1881, p. 251.
121 Brown, 1900, p. 72.
122 Ibid.

HOW MANY LIVES WERE LOST?

DESCRIPTIONS AND HISTORIES OF THE TEMECULA MASSACRE postulate a total ranging from thirty to forty deaths. This is an inaccurate reflection of all the historical evidence. These numbers appear to have originated from the accounts of the Mormon Battalion who arrived several weeks after the Massacre; the estimate may have been derived from the number they saw collected to be buried at the Temecula Cemetery. There were events and atrocities that the Mormon Battalion would not have borne witness to and could not have known that increased the number of slain warriors substantially. It is certain, for instance, that this number does not reflect the eighteen to twenty prisoners Juan Antonio killed after the battle, nor those who were buried in the canyon itself, those cremated in other locations, those taken by animals in the weeks that passed prior to the Battalion's arrival, or those whose bodies were lost in the flooding episode that occurred January 23-24, 1847.

Figure 25. "Indian Graveyard at Temecula" Seaver Center for Western History Research, Los Angeles County Museum of Natural History, Image SCWHR-P-002.2-2426R.

In January 1847, there were two full moons. Not only is January typically one of the coldest months of the year in Temecula, but the lunar activity would have resulted in increased animal activity. As a result of this, the bodies left in the canyon were widely dispersed throughout the area by scavengers. José David (Sargento) Rodriguez, a prominent Pechanga Tribal member, was interviewed several times in 1937 by one of John Harrington's assistants and prominent political leader from the Soboba reservation, Adan Castillo.

In one of these interviews, Sargento provides a first-hand account of the massacre. Being a small boy when the massacre occurred, he recounts specific information and details not found in any other sources. According to Sargento, "coyotes ate the bones of the people," which were collected in a wagon and buried in "a big [mass] grave" at the cemetery.[123] It is believed that some victims may have been buried near where they were killed, or in other mass graves within the battlefield corridor. Archaeological evidence suggests burial and cremation sites recently identified within the corridor may be related to this event. Mormon Battalion Private Robert Whitworth described the floodwaters in Aguanga as "waist-deep" on the night they camped near the canyon.[124] The power of the floodwaters and erosion would have dispersed the remains even further than the canyon itself.

Figure 26: José David "Sargento" Rodriguez, Pechanga Elder and Religious Leader, 1940. William Pink Collection, Pechanga Cultural Resources Department.

123 John P. Harrington Sound Recordings, National Anthropological Archives, Smithsonian Institution. Recording #1506, Interview with Sargento Rodriguez, Interviewed by Adam Castillo. Recorded August 10, 1937.

124 Whitworth, Robert W., Diary, Manuscript, 1846-1847, Bancroft Library, pp. 93-94.

Another factor that has contributed to the historical minimization of the number killed originates from Thomas Savage's description of Lugo's mental state when he interviewed him in 1877. Savage, evidently agitated that he was unable to obtain a wide variety of information to bolster his contracted pages for Bancroft, cites Lugo's "ignorance" and "feebleness in both body and mind."[125] Savage's remarks were used to discredit Lugo's own assessment of "perhaps a hundred Indians perished" as a mere exaggeration from an old and ailing man.[126] However, Lugo's accounts of the Battle of Chino and the Temecula Massacre are largely consistent with other accounts from the period.

At the time of Savage's interview, Lugo was sixty-four years old and reflecting upon events from his early thirties. Furthermore, Sargento Rodriguez's 1937 oral history interview substantiates that 100 people were killed. An analysis of census data taken from 1852 and 1860, and church records from 1820 to 1849, corroborates an approximate population loss of forty percent, placing the number killed in the massacre at around 100 people.[127] According to the 1860 census records in the Temecula Village, only 145 people remained who would have been alive during the time of the Temecula Massacre; meanwhile, the population of the Temecula Village in 1846 prior to the massacre was between 250 to 300 people.

---

125 Beattie, 1950, p. 186.

126 Ibid.

127 Analysis of baptismal register index data from January 1820 to December 1849 and census records from 1852 and 1860 kept on file at the Pechanga Cultural Resources Archives from the Phillip Crosthewaite and Dr. Lowell John Bean papers. See also, U.S., Indian Census Rolls, 1885-1940.

THE TEMECULA MASSACRE CEMETERY: PÁVKUN

THE REMAINS OF THE VICTIMS FROM the Massacre were brought to the Temecula Valley for burial from the battlefield which extends from the present day Vail Lake region all the way to Aguanga, which is located ten miles to the south. Pávkun, the location of the Temecula Massacre Cemetery may have already been an established burial or cremation site for the Temecula people, despite an 1867 source indicating it was a "new grave yard."[128]

Funds to consecrate the cemetery were amassed in 1867, and in May of that year, the San Bernardino *Guardian* reported, "We understand the citizens in locality set on foot a subscription, from

128 Parker, Horace, *The Historic Valley of Temecula: The Temecula Massacre*. Paisano Press, Balboa Island, CA, 1971; Hallaran, Kevin, Allene Archibald, Lowell J. Bean, and Sylvia B. Vane, *The Indian Cemetery at Old Temecula*, Manuscripts on file, Eastern Information Center, University of California, Riverside; Bruce Love, 1994, *Archaeological Field Inspection and Site Recording at the Old Temecula Cemetery (CA-RIV-115/H)*. Manuscripts on file, Eastern Information Center, University of California, Riverside; Bruce Love and Bai "Tom" Tang, 2002, *Historical Data on the Dimensions of the Indian Cemetery at Old Temecula*.

Figure 27. "Temecula Massacre" painting by Eddie Carey, courtesy of the artist. Reproduction archived at Pechanga Cultural Resources Department.

the proceeds of which they enclosed the graveyard with a neat and substantial fence. A very creditable proceeding certainly." In June 1867, an unnamed priest wrote to Bishop Amat of the Los Angeles Diocese describing the graveyard and asking for permission to consecrate the cemetery. The priest details the cemetery as being arranged nicely and that many people expressed desires to have it blessed.[129]

In the years following the massacre, the cemetery was recorded on several occasions. Many describe the cemetery's size between 150 to 180 square feet and having a low adobe perimeter wall with a wooden gate, a large wooden cross in the center, and a number of smaller crosses marking graves throughout. However, the size of the cemetery, circa 1847, cannot be ascertained from archival and literary sources alone. An adobe wall enclosure was constructed before 1867 and it is unknown if all the burials were located within.[130] Cremation was traditionally practiced and still occurring in 1847 but would have taken place outside of the cemetery, then brought later for internment.

129 Ibid.
130 Love, et al., 2002.

Figure 28. Temecula Cemetery, 1901. Note 'Éxva Teméeku, the creation mountain in the background. University of Southern California. Libraries and California Historical Society. Digitally reproduced by the USC Digital Library, 'Cemetery in Temecula where Ramona Waited while Alessandro went to the Wolfe Store to Sell his Violin, Ca. 1901,' CHS-753; USC-1-1-1-14072.

Archaeological surveys of the Temecula Indian Cemetery further established the known boundaries of the site. In 1989, archaeologists stated that the undisturbed cemetery mound measured approximately twenty-by-twenty meters.[131] For reasons unknown, this estimate of the mound's size is significantly smaller than any other record. In 1990, after human remains were discovered outside the known cemetery boundary, representatives of the Pechanga Cultural Resources Committee and the property owners reached an agreement to delineate the temporary boundaries of the cemetery with "the northern boundary to be established 10 meters north of the mound, 30 meters west of the mound, 30 meters south of the mound, and 80 meters east

131 Hallaran, et al., 1991.

Figure 29. A 1939 aerial photograph depicting cemetery with an intact perimeter wall. c-5750_205-32, 1939. Courtesy of University of California, Santa Barbara Library Geospatial Collection.

of the mound."[132]

In 1880, Alfred Perry Walbridge described the cemetery this way:

> About 4 o'clock, we arrived at Temecula, and I was very much disappointed in not seeing a fertile valley with trees and grass and houses. On the contrary, there is a

132 Pink, William and Gary Caldwell, Pauba Field Survey, 5-12-90. Manuscripts provided by William Pink. As cited in *Historical Data on the Dimensions of the Indian Cemetery at Old Temecula*, by Bruce Love and Bai "Tom" Tang, 2002.

Figure 30. A 1953 aerial photograph depicting cemetery mound. axm-1953b_1k-173, 1953. Courtesy of University of California, Santa Barbara Library Geospatial Collection.

store kept by Mr. Wolf, a school house, and two or three other houses, no verdure of any kind. The old Indian village on the hill has gone to ruin, and there are only a few old adobe walls standing. The Indians are scattered in different directions—few remain here. We passed the old Indian Grave Yard, which is enclosed by a 'dobe [sic] wall about 4 ft. high, and 50 yds. square. The graves all head to the North, and are marked by small crosses. A

> large cross has stood in the center, but the cross-bar has since fallen to the ground and nothing but a decayed post remains. Here is a collection of the best Indians that I ever saw.[133]

Figure 31. A 1976 aerial photograph depicting cemetery mound. Ami-RIV-76A Frame 8436, 1953. Courtesy of University of California, Santa Barbara Library Geospatial Collection.

133 Walbridge, Alfred Perry, n.d., Diary kept by A.P. Walbridge on a trip from Santa Ana, California to Arizona, October 11, 1880. (Emphasis added.)

Walbridge specifically calls out that the "graves all head to the North." This statement has a nuanced significance. Among the most consistent features of Catholic cemeteries during this period is their rectilinear layout with graves facing east. Common to Judeo-Christian tradition, graves are aligned on an east-to-west axis, with feet oriented to the east, so that the dead might face their Maker on Judgment Day.[134] Only in rare circumstances would specific graves be oriented in another direction, most often being clergy or members of significance. The sight of a graveyard with wooden crosses arranged to face north would have been perceived as an unusual circumstance, worthy of noting. Within the Luiseño culture, however, north is a sacred direction, and the pattern evidenced in the Temecula Cemetery aligns with burial practices still held within the Tribe today. The Temecula Indian Cemetery demonstrates a unique cohesion of cultures and burial practices.

The 1884 novel *Ramona,* written by Helen Hunt Jackson, brought the cemetery into popular culture. The novel describes the cemetery as abandoned wherein thieves have stolen the wooden gate for fuel.[135] Jackson was inspired to write Ramona after her visits to Southern California, officially to report on the condition of the Indians. Through congressional testimony, she was instrumental in assisting with the establishment of the Pechanga Indian Reservation in 1882.

Later accounts of the Temecula Indian Cemetery by land surveyors, authors, travelers, residents, and archaeologists convey the changes the land has undergone and how the cemetery faded from the landscape. When the cemetery was established, wooden grave markers were nearly universal in California. However, by the turn of the century only a few of these markers remained visible and intact. The area surrounding the area was irrigated for cultivation in the late

134 Meyer, Richard E., *Ethnicity and the American Cemetery.* Bowling Green State University Press, Ohio. 1993.

135 Jackson, Helen Hunt, *Ramona*. Grosset and Dunlap Publishers, New York. 1884.

Figure 32. View of cemetery in 1996, southwest. The low rise in the background with the cluster of trees is the location of the Temecula Village. Photo by Darell Farnbach.

1910s, and although the cemetery itself was avoided, the grading and leveling of the soil created the cemetery's appearance as a mound.

Aerial photographs from the twentieth century further reveal these changes.[136] In 1939, the cemetery mound was surrounded by agricultural fields and still had an intact perimeter wall. By 1947, the adobe wall had deteriorated but the cemetery mound is clearly differentiated from the agricultural fields and 1962 and 1976 aerial photographs show the cemetery mound and disking scar patterns, clearly avoiding the area. Former Vail Ranch employees Louis Roripaugh and James "Sandy" Vail Wilkinson also mentioned that the cemetery mound was avoided by the ranch agricultural operations.[137] Locals and ranch workers referred to the pasture itself as "Cemetery

136 Historic Aerials, 2020, electronic database: https://www.historicaerials.com/, accessed August 28, 2020; University of California, Santa Barbara (UCSB), Special Collections Library, Aerial Photography, multiple dates.

137 Hallaran, et al. 1991: 55; p. 70.

Field."[138] During the 1960s, the cemetery was often subject to flooding. Animal activity has periodically exposed remains. On one occasion, Roripaugh stated he saw what appeared to be a forearm bone, which he reburied in place.

Between 1995 and 2002, development of the surrounding areas accelerated. Wolf Store Road located to the south of the cemetery and Temecula Parkway to the north were widened and paved.[139] In 2005, the surrounding area was completely paved over for use as parking lots and developed for commercial use. It was during this time that the cemetery was capped with fill and enclosed by a perimeter fence.

Photographs of the cemetery from 1996 show the headstone of George Cuishman enclosed by metal pipes. The barrier was installed to prevent heavy equipment damage. The Cuishman grave is inscribed with the words, "George Cuishman, Died April 20, 1882, Aged 56 years."

George Cuishman may have been a miner in El Dorado County in 1852 who later came to Southern California.[140] By 1860, Cuishman is listed as a laborer in Warner Springs, and before 1870 had moved to Temecula, and in 1880 risen to the post of overseer for a Temecula farmer named Charles Thomas.[141] Alejandre Cuishman and his wife Jacoba are also recorded on the 1897 and 1902 Indian Census rolls for Pechanga. Alejandre was a descendant of George Cuishman who married a Temecula Indian woman. Roripaugh also noted an "Alex" Cuishman, worked as a ranch hand for the Vail Ranch during the 1930s or 1940s, who he described as an Indian.[142]

In a 1991 interview, Roripaugh describes how he caught a group of cowboys dragging the stone from the cemetery to the ranch head-

---

138 Oral history interview of Louis Roripaugh conducted by Eileen Archibald, January 13, 1991. Temecula Valley Historical Museum.

139 Historic Aerials, 2020.

140 Hallaran, 1991, p. 19.

141 *Press Enterprise*, "The Mystery of a Missing Tombstone." September 18, 1996.

142 Hallaran, 1991, 20. See also, Oral history interview of Louis Roripaugh conducted by Eileen Archibald, January 13, 1991. Temecula Valley Historical Museum.

Figure 33: Aerial view of Temecula Cemetery in 2022. Extensive development has occurred on all sides. Pechanga Cultural Resources Department.

quarters and he ordered them to return it.[143] Because of this incident, Roripaugh installed a pipe fence around the marker, but stated that he was unsure if it was in its proper place.[144] In September 1996, the headstone was reportedly stolen again.[145] It was later recovered, and is currently located within the Pechanga reservation.

The City of Temecula deeded the cemetery parcel to the Pechanga Tribe who now oversee the upkeep of the grounds. Tikithíkkish, known as "candle lighting," is the practice of placing lit candles at the graves of family members to honor their lives. This custom is still conducted annually at the cemetery on All Souls Day, November 2nd. These practices stem from traditional observances that have influences from Catholic ceremonies, similar to what is known as Day of the Dead in Mexico. Candle lighting is a way for the modern Native

143 Ibid.
144 Ibid.
145 *Press Enterprise*, 1996.

Figure 34: Temecula Cemetery in the middle of a shopping center, now behind a prefab wall. Pechanga Cultural Resources Department, 2020.

community to connect with recently deceased family members and ancestors from long ago.

Ultimately, the Temecula Massacre site and the Temecula Indian Cemetery are irreplaceable cultural landscapes strongly associated with the collective consciousness of the Pechanga people and continue to play significant roles as traditional sacred sites. The devastation and loss of up to a third of the village population was immense, effecting the Tribal community and future generations. The decades following the Temecula Massacre were further wrought with devastation and loss, with the eviction of the Temecula people from their village and the introduction of oppression and forced assimilation from the Americans.

Sadly, the Temecula Massacre was just the precursor to a long series of events that the Temecula people were subjected to by the newly formed state of California. Policies and procedures introduced to California Tribes by the U.S. federal government were aimed at eradicating, dispossessing, and assimilating the indigenous people of the state. While many Tribes in other parts of the country experienced colonization over a long period of time, the Tribes in California had mere decades to adapt to the governing polices of multiple countries; Spain, by introduction of colonization through the missions, Mexico and its localized ranchero administration, and the United States' ideology of removal and extermination. Despite this, California Tribal people survived these eras and are thriving communities today.

It has not been until recently that Tribes have had the resources to research, document, protect, and preserve important Tribal cultural and historic sites. This responsibility includes retelling the history from Tribal perspectives and a Native voice and including important sources such as oral accounts that have been passed through the generations. This work combines the scattered historic accounts found in diaries, letters, and scant published sources with the Tribal oral history providing a complete narrative of this devastating event, not only for the Pechanga Tribe but for the local community and scholars of California history.

CONCLUSION

THE INTENTION OF THIS BOOK IS to shed light on one of many important aspects of California history which is largely overlooked in historical narratives; the colonization and the subjugation of the West. The Native peoples of California played an important role in all aspects of the State's history, from being the object of Spanish colonization and missionization in creating neophytes and obedient subjects, to becoming the labor force of the large Mexican Ranchos, and ultimately a 'problem' to be dealt with under American Statehood. The Mexican-American War made Tribal people into pawns, pitted between two countries struggling for land and political gain. Sadly, throughout all of these eras the Native people lost: lives, land, social organization, language, and culture.

This book provides the reader with Tribal history and information not previously shared publicly, about the Temecula Massacre, the importance of the Battlefield Landscape, and the significance of the Temecula Cemetery to the Pechanga People today. This is the story of one event that greatly affected the Temecula Indians and is largely left out of the mainstream historical narrative. Much of the previous documentation concerning the Temecula Massacre is from non-Native perspectives. Often the Mexican-American War battles and skirmishes outside of California, such as *The Alamo* and *Battle of San*

Jacinto, garner more attention in the history books, largely due to the relative effortless defeat of the Californios by the Americans. During war, success is largely measured by loss of life, and the consensus in the history books is that the Americans lost the Battle of San Pasqual, which is deemed the "bloodiest battle of the war in California." Tragically, the Indian casualties of the Temecula Massacre are disregarded and treated as a cursory event of the overall campaign, not valid enough to be considered in the historical narrative as part of the war.

Up until this time, information about the Massacre and all events surrounding it were found in scattered reports about the Battle of San Pasqual, but never as a widely published focal piece. Oral accounts from Tribal sources include different perspectives of how and why the Massacre occurred, which include references about the betrayal of the neighboring Cahuilla Tribe, the fear and uncertainty of being in the middle of a war between the Mexicans and Americans, and sadly the inability to retrieve and bury loved ones killed in the ambush in a timely manner. It was important to the Pechanga Tribe to compile all of these sources and provide a well-rounded historical account.

Sadly, the Temecula Massacre was just a precursor to other tragic events for the Tribal community. In 1875, the people were evicted from the Temecula Village, of which the Cemetery was associated. Not only did the people have to leave their homes, but they also left their love ones buried there. Six years after the eviction, the Pechanga Reservation was established by Executive Order and the people were placed on this desolate reserve that had limited running water. The United States Government enacted additional debilitating and oppressive policies to further subjugate Native Peoples, including the implementation of off-reservation boarding schools, prohibiting religious observances and social gatherings, and closely monitoring daily life. This series of historic events continues to affect the Tribe today.

While population decline and erosion of Tribal social organization began with the first Spanish colonizers, the Temecula Massacre was a catastrophic event that had an immediate and significant impact on the Tribal community. In one day, over a third of the Village population was strategically and brutally murdered, at a time when daily life was already enmeshed by turmoil and uncertainty. This large loss of life deeply affected the community structure starting with the political and religious leadership, and medical and spiritual healers, to the core social organization. The Eviction and the establishment of the reservation further fractured the community by forcing people to have to choose between remaining and struggling to survive or to leave the valley to find work to support their families. Within another decade, boarding schools began taking children away from parents, causing multiple generations of culturally marginalized adults, who were forcibly disenfranchised from their communities and culture. Additional Federal Indian polices continued to pressure Tribal communities to assimilate, by terminating Tribes and relocating families to large cities far away from reservations. Unfortunately, the Pechanga community was affected by these assimilation strategies, in the 1960s there were under a dozen people living on the reservation. Despite these federal policies and measures to oppress Tribal culture, the Pechanga Tribal community experienced a resurgence of pride and investment in the reservation beginning in the 1970s and 1980s with the establishment of formalized membership and Tribal programs. Later, with the introduction of gaming in California, Tribal Members returned to work and live on the reservation and Pechanga has become one of the most politically powerful Tribes in California and the Nation.

For 187 years, the Native people of Temecula Valley watched over the Cemetery, making sure it was not disturbed by farming or desecration. For the most part, it was left alone and respected by non-Native pioneer families. However, during the development boom of the 1990s the Cemetery boundaries were threatened, and the Pechanga Band of Indians began negotiations with the City of Temecula for long-term preservation. To meet this objective, Pechanga Cultural Resources investigators conducted research, analysis, and field surveys to document the history of its use and the extent of the boundaries. As part of the research and evaluation, the Temecula Massacre Cemetery was found eligible for listing on the National Register of Historic Places.

The Temecula Cemetery continues to be an important sacred place to the Pechanga people. With economic stability and investment in Cultural Resource management and protection by Tribal Members and Leadership, Pechanga can actively endeavor to protect sacred places and landscapes, including Pu'éska Mountain, the place of Tribal Creation and the Temecula Cemetery, the last visible tie to the Massacre. The Pechanga Tribe will continue to care for this special place and with this work, aspire to revive the fading memories of the Temecula Massacre.

INDEX OF FIGURES

REFERENCES

Bailey, Lynn Robinson, *Bosque Redondo: An American concentration Camp.* Socio-Technical Books, Pasadena. 1970.

Beebe, Rose Marie and Robert Senkewicz, "On the Road to San Diego: Junípero Serra's Baja California Diary." *Journal of San Diego History,* 59(4):180-240. 2013.

Beattie, George William, "The Battle of Chino." *The Quarterly: Historical Society of Southern California* (1942) 24 (4): 143–160. 1942.

Beattie, Helen Pruitt, "Life of a Rancher by Don José Carmen Lugo" as told to Thomas Savage, 1877. *Historical Society of Southern California Quarterly,* Volume 32, Number 3, pp 185-236. 1950.

Bell, Horace, *On the Old West Coast: Being Further Reminiscences of a Ranger, Major Horace Bell.* W. Morrow & Co. 1976.

Benton, Thomas Hart Benton, "Nomination of General Kearny: Substance of the Speech of Mr. Benton, of Missouri, In the Senate – Executive Session," July 1848, from *The Congressional Globe for the First Session, Thirtieth Congress: Containing Speeches and Important State Papers,* Blair and Rives: Washington. 1848.

Bibb, Leland E., William Marshall "The Wickedest Man in California," *The Journal of San Diego History,* San Diego Historical Society Quarterly, Winter 1976, Vol. 22, No. 1. 1976.

Pablo Apis and Temecula, *The Journal of San Diego History,* San Diego Historical Society Quarterly, Fall 1991, Volume 37, Number 4.

Bliss, Robert, Robert Bliss Journal, MS 79, San Diego History Center Document Collection, San Diego, CA. 1846.

Brown, James S., *Life of a Pioneer: The Autobiography of James S. Brown.* Salt Lake City: Cannon & Sons Co. 1900.

Carrico, Richard, *Strangers in a Stolen Land: Indians of San Diego County from Prehistory to the New Deal.* Sunbelt Publications. 2008.

Cooke, Phillip St., *Report from the Secretary of War, communicating, in compliance with a resolution of the Senate, of the 21st February, 1849, a copy of the official journal of Lieutenant Colonel Philip St. George Cooke, from Santa Fe to San Diego,* United States Congress Senate. 1849.

The Conquest of New Mexico and California in 1846-1848, Chicago: Rio Grande Press. 1878.

Dunn, Dana Ruth Hicks, *Strategies for Survival: Indian Transitions in the Mountains of San Diego County, 1846 – 1907.* Dissertation, University of California, Riverside, Department of History. 2013.

Ellison, William Henry, *The Life and Adventures of George Nidever 1802-1883.* McNally & Loftin, Publishers, Santa Barbara. 1984.

Frémont, John Charles, *Memoirs of My Life.* Chicago: Belford, Clarke & Co. 1887.

Griffin, John S., *A Doctor Comes to California.* San Francisco: California Historical Society, 1953.

Guinn, James Miller, *A History of California and an Extended History of Los Angeles and Environs,* Historical Record Company: Los Angeles, California. 1915.

Hallaran, Kevin B., *Historical Background of the Old Temecula Village Indian Cemetery,* in The Indian Cemetery at Old Temecula, report prepared for Jerry Swanger, Sr. Vail Properties. Report in possession of authors. 1991.

Hallaran, Kevin, Allene Archibald, Lowell J. Bean, and Sylvia B. Vane, *The Indian Cemetery at Old Temecula,* report prepared for Jerry Swanger, Sr. Vail Properties. Report in possession of authors. Manuscripts on file, Eastern Information Center, University of California, Riverside. 1991.

Hancock, Levi Ward, *The Saving Sacrifice of the Mormon Battalion from the Journals of Levi Ward Hancock.* Herbert A. Hancock eds. Bystander at Large Productions: Utah. 2000.

Harlow, Neal, *California Conquered: The Annexation of a Mexican Province 1846-1850.* University of California Press, Berkeley. 1982.

Harrington, John Peabody, John P. Harrington Sound Recordings, National Anthropological Archives, Smithsonian Institution. Recording #1506, Interview with Sargento Rodriguez, Interviewed by Adam Castillo. Recorded August 10, 1937.

The John Peabody Harrington Papers 1907-1959. National Anthropological Archives, Smithsonian Institution. 1986.

Hayes, Benjamin, "Pioneer Notes from the Diaries of Judge Benjamin Hayes, 1849-1875: Chapter VIII, Later San Diego Notes, Massacre of Pauma," American Memory, Library of Congress. 1875.

Hicks, Sam, "Temecula Tragedy," The High Country, Vol 12, pp. 42-48. 1970.

Hine, Robert V. and John Mack Faragher, *Frontiers: A Short History of the American West.* Yale University Press: New Haven. 2007.

Historic Aerials, Electronic database: https://www.historicaerials.com, accessed August 28, 2020.

Hollon, Cory S., "A Leap in the Dark" The Campaign to Conquer New Mexico and California, 1846–1847," *Army History,* Winter 2015, No. 94. 2015.

Hudson, Millard F., "The Pauma Massacre." *The Southern California Quarterly,* Vol 7, Number 1, pp.13-21. 1906.

Jackson, Helen Hunt, *Ramona.* Grosset and Dunlap Publishers, New York. 1884.

Jackson, Robert H. and Edward Castillo, *Indians, Franciscans, and Spanish Colonization: The Impact of the Mission System on California Indians.* University of New Mexico Press, Albuquerque. 1995.

James, Harry C., *The Cahuilla Indians.* Westlake Press. 1960.

Jasper, James, "The Wickedest Man in California," *Los Angeles Times Magazine,* August 2, 1931, pp. 11,14. 1931.

Jones, Nathaniel V., Nathaniel V. Jones Journal with the Mormon Battalion. 1847. Utah Historical Quarterly Volume I-VI, pp. 6-24. 1847.

Lech, Steve, *Along the Old Roads: A History of the Portion of Southern California That Became Riverside County 1772-1893.* Published by author. 2004.

Love, Bruce, *Archaeological Field Inspection and Site Recording at the Old Temecula Cemetery (CA-RIV-115/H).* Manuscripts on file, Eastern Information Center, University of California, Riverside. 1994.

Love, Bruce and Bai "Tom" Tang, *Historical Data on the Dimensions of the Indian Cemetery at Old Temecula.* 2002.

Lugo, Don José del Carmen, *Vida de Un Ranchero.* Interview by Thomas Savage. Original manuscript, Bancroft Library, University of California, Berkeley. 1877.

McCown, Benjamin Ernest, *Collected Papers of Benjamin Ernest McCown,* Paper Number Six. "Archaeological Survey of Pauba Flood Control Basin." Archaeological Survey Association of Southern California. 1964.

Meyer, Richard E., *Ethnicity and the American Cemetery.* Bowling Green State University Press, Ohio. 1993.

Miller, Anne J., "María Antonia Apis: A Young Luiseño Indian Woman." *Southern California Quarterly* Vol. 86, No. 2, pp. 113-126. 2004.

The Southern Emigrant Trail through Riverside County. Author House: Bloomington, IN. 2012.

Monnette, Orra Eugene, "Fort Moore and the Battle of San Pasqual." *Annual Publication of the Historical Society of Southern California,* Vol. 12, No. 3 (1923), pp. 42-52. 1923.

Morrison, Lorrin L., *Warner: The Man and the Ranch.* Published by Author: Los Angeles, CA. 1962.

Parker, Horace, The Brush Country Journal. *Riverside Daily Press,* Part 11: Temecula. October 14, p. 38. 1956. Part 15: Temecula, November 9. 1956. Part 16: Temecula, November 16. 1956. Epilogue to Temecula Massacre, December 2, p. 14. 1956.

The Historic Valley of Temecula: The Temecula Massacre. Balboa Island, CA: Paisano Press, 1971.

"The Temecula Massacre." *Westerners Brand Book Number 10,* 176-88. Los Angeles: Los Angeles Corral No. 10, 1963.

Peet, Mary Rockwood, *San Pasqual: A Crack in the Hills.* Culver City, Calif.: Highland Press, 1949. 1949.

Phillips, George Harwood, *Chief and Challengers: Indian Resistance and Cooperation in Southern California, 1769-1906.* University of California Press, Berkeley. 1975.

Popper, Virginia S., Change and Persistence: Mission Neophyte Foodways at Selected Colonial Alta California Institutions, *Journal of California and Great Basin Anthropology* Vol. 36, No. 1, pp. 5-25. 2016.

Riverside Daily Press (Press Enterprise), "The Mystery of a Missing Tombstone." September 18, 1996.

Reading, James, "Jean Baptiste Charbonneau," *Journal of San Diego History,* San Diego Historical Society Quarterly, March 1965, Volume 11, Number 2. 1965.

Regan, Geoffrey, *SNAFU: Great American Military Disasters,* Avon Books. 1993.

Roberts, Elizabeth Judson, *Indian Stories of the Southwest.* San Francisco: Harr Wagner Publishing Co. 1917.

Sabin, Edward Legrand, *Kit Carson Days, 1809-1868: Adventures in the Path of Empire, Volume 2.* University of Nebraska Press: Lincoln, reprint 1995. 1935.

Smythe, William Ellsworth, History of San Diego, 1542-1908. San Diego: History Co., 1907.

Sparkman, Philip Stedman, *The Culture of the Luiseño Indians,* University of California Publications in American Archaeology and Ethnology, Vol. 8(4):187-23. 1908.

Standage, Henry, Diary of Henry Standage, Company "E," Mormon Battalion. Manuscripts on file, San Diego Historical Society Research Archives.

Strong, William Duncan, University of California Publications in *American Archaeology and Ethnology*, Volume 26. 1929.

Twitchell, Ralph Emerson, The History of the Military Occupation of New Mexico. Smith Books Co. 1909.

Tyler, Sergeant Daniel, *A Concise History of the Mormon Battalion in the Mexican War 1846-1847.* Salt Lake City. 1881.

Walbridge, Alfred Perry, Diary kept by A.P. Walbridge on a Trip from Santa Ana, Cal., to Arizona.

Walker, Dale L., *Bear Flag Rising: The Conquest of California, 1846.* Tom Doherty Associates. 1999.

Whitworth, Robert W., Diary, manuscript, 1846-1847, Bancroft Library. 1846-1847.

Woodward, Arthur, *Lances at San Pascual.* Westgate Press, Oakland. 1948.

United States Congress, Senate. 1887. *Journal of the Executive Proceedings of the Senate of the United States of America,* From December 1, 1845, to August 14, 1848, Inclusive. Vol. VII. Government Printing Office: Washington. 1887.

ABOUT THE AUTHORS

GARY DUBOIS, JD, MSW, MA is the Founding Director of the Pechanga Band of Indians, Cultural Resources Department and the Tribal Historic Preservation Officer (THPO) for the Tribe. DuBois earned a Juris Doctorate from Washington University Law School. He is a scholar of Native American History, The American West, and Constitutional Law, and is a lecturer in these fields at California State University San Bernardino. DuBois clerked for the Cherokee Nation of Oklahoma Tribal Courts and was a Udall Fellow for the United States Senate Indian Affairs Committee. A veteran of the United States Army, DuBois served over fifteen years in the Army National Guard with active duty from 2004 to 2006 as an infantry squad leader. Gary DuBois is an enrolled citizen of the Pechanga Band of Indians.

LISA WOODWARD, PH.D. is the Archivist for the Pechanga Band of Indians, Cultural Resources Department. She earned her doctoral degree in Native American Studies from University of California, Davis. As archivist, Woodward manages the Tribe's collection of photographs, archival documents, ephemera, and sound recordings. While at Davis as an undergraduate and later graduate student, she assisted in developing the J.P. Harrington Database

Project, which assisted in providing Tribal Communities access to John Harrington's extensive collection of field notes on Native languages. She also actively conducts research for the Tribe in the areas of Cultural Resource Management and Collection repatriation from institutions across the country.